Hannah Robinson
& Rachel Howard

Londoni is full of fashionable restaurants and bars, their turnover fuelled by a relentless PR machine that tells locals where to go to see and be seen. This guide is an antidote to food fads, molecular mixologists and celebrity chefs who have morphed into multinational brands. It's a collection of unusual places in unlikely locations, independent businesses kept afloat by eccentric owners, local institutions oblivious to passing trends.

Welcome to the second edition of London's least hyped restaurants, cafées, bars, and clubs, with over 60 brand-new entries. As before, the food and drink isn't always the most memorable thing about these places. They are for people who love to explore as much as to eat interesting food. Some are expensive, some are humble. Their diversity – a Somali village restaurant, an Italian Marseillaise fondue joint, a Brixton communal fridge – reflects the cosmopolitan spirit of London, a city that champions the unconventional despite being steeped in tradition.

It took a long time to whittle down the final selection, aided by many intrepid dining and drinking partners, whose curiosity, enthusiasm and tolerance for bad meals knew no bounds (we hope they will recognise themselves in these pages). Many of the original finds from the first edition are still so brilliant and remain so defiantly undiscovered that we had to keep them in, amending the write-ups to reflect their latest peculiarities – though we are pleased to report that several haven't so much as re-patched a cushion cover.

Hidden amongst the chapters you will find a few 'Easter Egg' surprises: collections of clandestine garden cafés, speakeasy bars, and even secret places to dance salsa – if you feel the need to burn off some of the calories you've been consuming. But we are sure there are many more unsung secrets in London that we've yet to discover and we'd love to hear your suggestions for the next edition.

Hannah Robinson & Rachel Howard

Don't hesitate to contact us:
E-mail: info@jonglezpublishing.com
Jonglez Publishing, 25 rue du Maréchal Foch
78000 Versailles, France

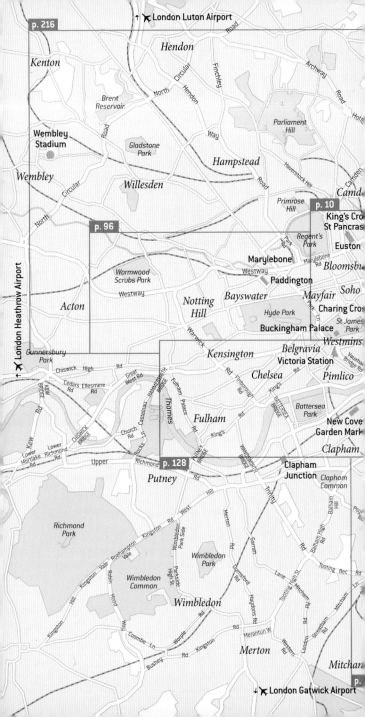

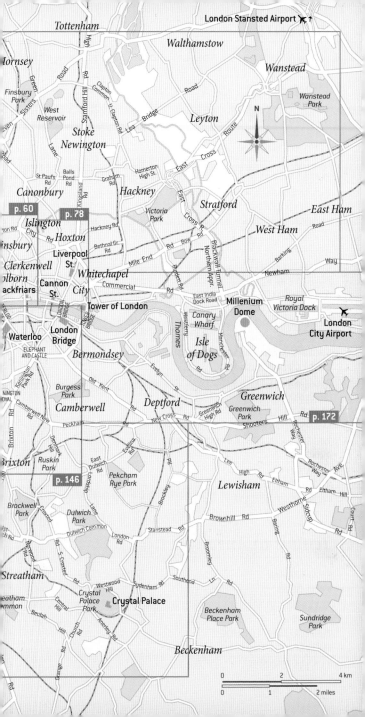

CONTENTS

Westminster to Camden

Temple to Angel

Tower Bridge to Shoreditch

Marylebone to Shepherd's Bush

CONTENTS

Westminster to Hammersmith

South Bank to Brixton

Whitechapel to Woolwich

Greater London South East

Greater London North & West

Westminster to Camden

AMERICAN BAR
AT THE STAFFORD HOTEL

An American friend

16–18 St James's Place, SW1A 1NJ
020 7493 0111
www.thestaffordlondon.com
reservations@thestaffordlondon.com
Daily 8am–12am
Tube station: Green Park

A shrine to a secret agent

Hiding among the offerings is a bust of former hotel resident Nancy Wake, a secret agent whose undercover work in the Second World War saved thousands of lives. Code-named "the White Mouse" by the Gestapo because she kept escaping them, she showed exceptional bravery in her work for the French Resistance and was the Allied forces' most decorated woman. New Zealand born Wake had been introduced to her first "bloody good drink" at the American Bar by the hotel's manager and fellow Resistance fighter, Louis Berdet. It was here that she celebrated her 90th birthday and lived out her days until she could no longer lift a cocktail glass. Now there is one named in her honour: the White Mouse cocktail. Bloody good it is too.

The Stafford Hotel is very discreetly situated within the heart of regal St James, the area surrounding Henry VII's Tudor palace – residence of the British royal family right up until the time of Queen Victoria. Approach on a well-heeled foot either via a pathway skirting the north-east side of Green Park or through a double archway between 64 and 68 St James's Street. This leads you into Blue Ball Yard, a cobbled ex-stable yard which has seen the clatter of many a royal filly. Now it is the garden for the Stafford Hotel's bar, perfect for a summer evening drink and a cigar. But it's when you pop inside for a top-up that you encounter the hotel's right royal peculiarity.

"American Bar" was the name given to many hotel bars during the 1930s to lure in wealthy transatlantic clientele with the promise of friendly service and proper cocktails. Guests at the Stafford felt so welcome that they started giving small tokens of their appreciation to the bar manager, Charles Guano. Starting with a little wooden Native American totem pole carving, the guests' generosity rapidly spun out of control and soon every inch of the bar's walls and ceilings were festooned with baseball caps, model aeroplanes, banner flags and celebrity signed photos. Dolly Parton, Bill Nighy and Gore Vidal wish you well. A large framed metal screwdriver commemorates a rookie error by a busboy who was still to learn his cocktail names.

A recent redesign has organised the chaos, brought more light and space into the bar and also introduced a new Mediterranean tapas style menu of delicious treats like spring pea croquettes with truffle aioli. But you can still find little hints of the old American romance: mini doughnuts with a crab & chilli stuffing, anyone?

A labyrinthine wine cellar for underground dining

Beneath the hotel is an even deeper secret: a vast wine cellar, built in the 1700s by Lord Francis Godolphin and thought to be London's oldest. Its long, dank, narrow corridors snake down past over 8,000 bottles of the world's finest wines, now carefully picked and guarded by Master Sommelier Gino Nardella. Reputedly one spur leads directly to the old palace, but my exploration eventually hit a cul-de-sac filled with propaganda posters, newspaper headlines, sandbags and helmets, commemorating its use as a wartime bomb shelter. At one point it widens out into a room where 17th-century wine barrels were once stored, now a private dining room which can seat up to 44 … ideal for a post-apocalyptic dinner party.

DUKES BAR

Undiluted pleasure

Dukes Hotel, 35 St James's Place SW1A 1NY
020 7491 4840
www.dukeshotel.com
bookings@dukeshotel.com
Monday–Saturday 2pm–11pm, Sunday and Bank Holidays 4pm–10.30pm
Tube station: Green Park or Piccadilly Circus

Since the first edition of this book was published, London has had a cocktail revolution. Down every nook and cranny of the city, you will find a hidden bar serving a themed cocktail list in luxuriously vintage surroundings (see page 86). But the place that invented this recipe before anyone thought to remix it was Dukes Bar. Hidden in a cul-de-sac off a cul-de-sac, it's almost impossible to stumble across. This is the bar where Alessandro Palazzi has developed a very distinctive way

of making martinis, inspired by the hotel's former visitor Ian Fleming and his James Bond books.

A cherry wood trolley is wheeled to our table. At the side, a row of little crystal jugs containing Alessandro's English vermouths, specially created by Sacred Spirits. On top, straight out of the freezer, are the glasses and alcohol. There is no ice and there is no shaking, not even any stirring; the idea is to keep the temperature as low as possible whilst ensuring absolutely no dilution. The spirits, thick from their sub-zero storage, are quickly poured into your glass; a wide leaf of zest is pared from an Amalfi lemon, twisted over and tucked into the side of the glass. And, with the air filled with the spritz of citrus oil, I sip what might be the strongest martini I have ever tasted.

I chose the "Tiger Tanaka", which has oriental notes of ginger and orange. My friend went off menu: she likes her martinis dirty, as she likes her, um, burgers. Alessandro gently persuades her to try his way, but gives her the bottle of brine on the side should she prefer hers. Apprehensive of the five measures of pure alcohol, I attempt to line my stomach from the bowls of large green olives, nuts and crackers, but after only a few sips I feel my brain sort of pleasantly … slide. We spend the next three hours in a very comfortable fug – talking intensely, while the staff discreetly refill our snack bowls (more than once). There is a limit of two cocktails per customer but we decide that, in this case, cocktails are not like breasts, they are like bartenders – if they're this good, you only need one.

The perfect bartender

Alessandro Palazzi has thirty years' experience in the top bars of the world, though for someone whose time and attention are in such high demand, he is surprisingly relaxed and chatty. He tells us he hates the term mixologist and is proud to be called a bartender, working in the hospitality industry: he serves customers, he doesn't perform. Over the years, he has tended bars in the most challenging locations, for the most glittering of stars: be it rock, political, business, military or screen. They don't faze him because, in his opinion, the real celebrities are doctors, soldiers, nurses. And he has distilled his experience into these essential lessons: Never judge a book by its cover. Never panic. Never stop learning. And that the personality of the bartender must include three ingredients: Diplomatic. Charismatic. And Acrobatic. As Alessandro manages to conduct the entire room while simultaneously telling us his career history and occasionally nipping off to personally attend to another guest, I realise that in him these spirits are mixed to perfection.

BERRY BROS & RUDD

A lot of bottle

3 St James's Street, SW1A 1EG
020 7022 8973
Check www.bbr.com for details of upcoming events
Shop hours: Monday–Friday 10am–9pm, Saturday 10am–5pm; closed
Sunday
Tube station: Green Park or Piccadilly Circus

Britain's oldest wine merchants, Berry Bros & Rudd have dispensed rare vintages to bon viveurs since 1698. Still a family business, the shop has barely changed since the Widow Bourne opened The Coffee Mill, selling spices, tea and coffee. The original scales have been used to weigh famous customers (including Lord Byron and Napoleon III) for 300 years. A secret tunnel, now blocked, linked the warren of cellars to St James' Palace, so royals could pay clandestine visits to the ladies of the night who frequented the shop. The shops cellars hold 100,000 bottles, but patrons' finest vintages – worth a staggering £650 million – are laid down in a warehouse in less romantic Basingstoke.

Today, the dramatically refurbished cellars are mainly used for wine tastings, luncheons, dinners and the wine school, open to all. More intimate events take place in a 17th-century townhouse on Pickering Place, a secret Georgian cul-de-sac adjacent to the shop, site of the country's last duel. A four-hour luncheon in the Long Room, an elegant

Photos by Joakim Blockstrom

vision of silk wallpaper and polished mahogany, is surely one of the most decadent ways to spend a Monday afternoon.

Contrary to expectation, a leisurely lunch designed as an introduction to Spanish wines was not remotely intimidating – and there's not a Rioja in sight. Our hosts are passionate, eloquent and witty. They take questions with genuine interest. Remarkably, they're just as articulate after sampling seven wines – though they wisely refrain from draining their glasses, unlike the rest of us.

We started with crisp Gramona cava, which brought a whiff of Mediterranean summer to drizzly London. Two contrasting whites from the coastal region of Galicia set off basil-crusted sardines with piquillo pepper salsa and Gordal olives stuffed with chorizo. The wines were exceptional but the food is no afterthought: chef Stewart Turner is a protégé of Michel Roux Jr. Slow-roast pork belly with pata negra and apple purée packed a punch, rather like the 2007 Pesquera Reserva ("Nothing like those Spanish head-bangers we used to know," as our host noted drily.) We savoured a 1996 Torresilo from Ribero del Duero slowly with a trio of Spanish cheeses, served with pan de higo, membrillo and oat biscuits. An ethereal macadamia nut parfait with prune spring rolls and Earl Grey jelly almost outshone a smooth, amber East India Solera sherry.

In centuries past, casks of sherry were lashed to ships sailing for the Indies as ballast. With all that extra ballast, thankfully we weren't subjected to a weigh-in on the shop scales on our way out.

Photo by Joakim Blockstrom

Blitz Spirits

13 Kingly Court, Carnaby Street W1B 5PG
020 7352 6200
cahoots-london.com
highspirits@cahoots-london.com
Monday—Wednesday 5pm—1am, Thursday 4pm—2am, Friday 4pm—3am,
Saturday 1pm—3am, Sunday 3pm—12am
Tube station: Oxford Circus or Piccadilly Circus

My companion suggests we dress up for the evening, so I gamely pull out my best Bletchley Park frock, curl my hair and rummage around for a stern handbag. She meets me in Boots on Carnaby Street dressed impressively in full Women's Voluntary Service uniform, which she doesn't get that many opportunities to air … though she has accessorised with knee-high black boots and a large holdall, so the outfit has taken on a sort of Nazi Stripper look. After being followed round Boots by the store detective and then taking several wrong turns in Kingly Court, we finally find the hidden entrance, labelled only "To the Trains". We give the doorman the secret password we've been sent with our booking and descend straight into 1946. Our vintage-lippied hostess greets us with a copy of the *Cahoots* newspaper and escorts us through the underground train station cum war shelter which has been tarted up, as they did back then, with homely knick-knacks – fringed

fabric lampshades, mini Union Jack flags and bunting triangles. The place is packed with revellers celebrating the end of the war, though most haven't made quite the effort we have, scoffs the Nazi Stripper, who has discovered that the top pocket of her WVS dress is an ideal mobile phone holder.

This place was once the Tatty Bogle, an out-of-hours drinking club opened by Scottish officers in 1917, and it later got used as a WWII air-raid shelter, so the theme is justified. We are seated inside a train carriage at a bench table bedecked with perforated tin candle holders and a can of peaches repurposed as a popcorn server. Water glasses are filled from an army green thermos. Our newspaper turns out to be an extensive cocktail menu, grouped into the social classes of the period. Nazi Stripper orders a "Vera Lynn" from the "Starlets & Sirens" column, while I plump for an earthier "Grow for Victory" from the "Landgirls & Homeguards" section. My cocktail is healthier and tastes better, but hers comes served inside Vera's green head and there's really no beating that.

The music isn't quite the right era – they're playing hyper electro-swing, which starts to grate after ooh, maybe eight bars – but apparently that's just Friday and Saturday nights. The bathrooms are (aptly) a relief, piping out gentle Cockney rhyming-slang lessons, "Parliamo Glasgow" style. We are probably more suited to weekend afternoons, when Saturday "Squiffy Picnic" hampers or Sunday "Cocktail Cuppas and Cakes" are accompanied by live crooners and swing bands. But maybe that's just our vintage.

BOB BOB RICARD

Subterranean opulence

1 Upper James Street, Soho, W1F 9DF
020 3145 1000
www.bobbobricard.com
reservations@bobbobricard.com
Monday—Wednesday 12.30pm—3pm and 6pm—12am, Thursday 12.30pm —
3pm and 5.30pm—12am, Saturday 12.30pm—3pm and 5.30pm—1am, Sunday
12.30pm—3pm and 5.30pm—12am
Tube station: Oxford Circus or Piccadilly Circus

I'm a sucker for a good booth. Bob Bob Ricard, which bills itself as a "diner-deluxe", is a glorious roomful of cobalt leather booths offset by clashing Art Deco wallpaper. Designed by David Collins, it's like a souped-up 1930s ocean liner with a dash of the Orient Express. There's a mottled marble bar where you can get sozzled on pink rhubarb gin and tonics alongside Soho's film execs.

If you're more partial to vodka and would rather not see and be seen, head down to the hidden basement bar. It's like a set from *Mad Men*.

You can picture Don Draper seducing his latest squeeze in one of the tall red leather booths (they're a tight fit, which adds to the intimate atmosphere.) Expertly mixed cocktails focus on British ingredients such as the BBR Botanical (Pimm's, Hendrick's gin, elderflower, sparkling wine).

Such opulence doesn't come cheap, but mark-ups on fine wines and champagnes are relatively modest, with margins capped at £50 per bottle. Top-class vodkas, all served at -18 degrees, are hand-picked by one of the two owners who hails from Russia – Leonid Shutov. After one too many dirty martinis, resist the urge to order caviar and blinis (unless Draper is paying). Matchstick chips and flaky tartlets with sophisticated toppings such as fig, honey and mascarpone will hit the spot.

Bobby's Bar is never oversubscribed and you won't have to fight to get to the bar, as standing room isn't allowed. Premium cocktails, proper booths, and a glamorous sanctuary from the Soho scrum: what more could you want?

Champagne on call

Every booth has a champagne button so you can summon more bubbly in the twinkling of an eye. The house champagne is Pol Roger, Winston Churchill's favourite. As he once said of his preferred tipple: "In victory, deserve it; in defeat, need it."

TRISHA'S BAR (NEW EVARISTO CLUB)

Old-school Soho hideout

57 Greek Street, Soho, W1D 3DX
020 7437 9536
www.facebook.com/TrishasSoho
Daily 5.30pm−1.30am
Tube station: Leicester Square or Tottenham Court Road

There aren't many members' clubs in Soho that are accessible to pretty much anyone, but this unpretentious dive is an exception. There's none of the exclusive veneer of celebrity haunts such as Soho House or The Groucho, and the basement bar is so small that there's no room for oversized egos.

It's not immediately obvious that there's a bar here at all. The entrance is through an unmarked door in a grotty building (the kind that normally advertises "Models Upstairs"). Look for the buzzer that says "Trisha/Evaristo Club". Although officially called the New Evaristo Club, most regulars know it as Trisha's (after the owner, Trisha Bergonzi), or as The Hideout. On weekends there's usually a doorman loitering outside, who can generally be sweet-talked into letting you in even if you're not a member. Sometimes they'll make you sign the guestbook and charge you a pound or two on the door; sometimes they'll just wave you through.

A sticky carpet leads downstairs to a room that's straight out of a 1960s mafia job. The walls are half-lined with mock-chalet wood panelling. The rest of the space is plastered in lime-green paint, photos of boxers, favoured patrons and Italian legends such as Frank Sinatra, Don Corleone and the Pope. There are a few rickety chairs and tables, and a small Formica bar from which the gnarled bar staff dispense cheap wine, warm beer and witty asides.

Arrive early or very late on weekends. After the surrounding pubs close, an assortment of random characters piles in – transvestites, hipsters, fashion students and elderly Italians who have long called this corner of Soho home. The occasional celebrity makes an appearance, but nobody seems to notice. If you're lucky, a jazz crooner or rock and roll band will squeeze into the corner and start jamming. There's no dance-floor but that doesn't stop the crowd from going wild.

They've added an extra toilet, so now there's two – but everything else remains the same, including the tiny smoking area at the back where you're bound to make friends, if not make out with someone. Anything goes.

NEARBY
Algerian Coffee Stores   ⑦
52 Old Compton Street, Soho, W1D 4PB
020 7437 2480
www.algcoffee.co.uk
Founded in 1887, this classic coffee emporium has preserved much of its stunning Victorian interior. As well as over 80 types of coffee, 120 teas, and all sorts of sweet treats to take home, they serve perhaps the finest – and certainly the cheapest – espresso and cappuccino in London at the worn wooden counter.

LA BODEGA NEGRA

Triple X Mexican

9 Old Compton Street, Soho, W1D 5JF
020 7758 4100
www.labodeganegra.com
info@labodeganegra.com
Monday–Saturday 5.30pm–1am, Sunday 6pm–12am
Tube station: Tottenham Court Road or Leicester Square

So you're standing outside what appears to be a sex shop at the end of Old Compton Street in Soho. A big neon open pink mouth licks its lips. A naked girl with her knickers round her knees. Live Nude! Adult Videos! Peep Show! Are you sure you're going in? Those huge neon eyes flutter their pink zigzag eyelashes, daring you to enter. Strip. Tease. The longer you hang around outside, the dodgier you seem. It's not really feasible to explain to everyone in the busy street that it's not what it looks like.

So you walk purposefully ahead and duck inside. There's a voluptuous sexy lady perched on a stool inside next to a dummy in a PVC gimp suit. This could be a horrible mistake. But thankfully when she sends you downstairs, you find yourself in a dark cavernous Mexican bar and restaurant. Day of the Dead skulls and tequila barrels peep out of the crumbling vaulted walls. One table has a fantastic disc-mirrored hemisphere curved over the end, like sitting inside a giant inverted mirror ball.

With such an eye-catching concept and designer interior, my old school friend and I are quite expecting the food to be less like sex and more Tex Mex average. But it's actually really good – contemporary pan-Latin American, full of fresh ingredients and exciting flavour bursts. Delicious and delicate lemon sole black *aguachile* – a ceviche with black garlic, serrano chilli and squid ink. A row of tiny soft tacos, some stuffed with crispy soft-shell crab with a smoky chipotle chilli cream, others with duck in a tangy tamarind sauce. Even the broccoli stems are perfectly succulent and spicy (can broccoli be described as sexy?).

Keeping up the theme, our handsome Latin waiter flirts heavily with us, attempting to lure us into tasting the agave cocktails and extensive tequila list. But we want to keep our brains intact for a fairly intense movie screening we're going to later (Lynne Ramsay's *You Were Never Really Here*), so we have the *michelada*, a beer with a tasty spiced tomato, salt and lime mix. It's early evening so the restaurant isn't that full, but you can tell it's the kind of place where people end up dancing on the tables, especially with such encouraging staff (our tequila-touting waiter is quite tenacious). We're glad we resisted him because the movie was amazing. But if you're not trying to stay sober, this is the place to come for a dark and tempting red-hot dinner.

LE BEAUJOLAIS

Grape expectations

25 Litchfield Street, Covent Garden, WC2H 9NJ
020 7836 2955
www.lebeaujolais.london
info@lebeaujolais.london
Monday—Friday 12pm—11pm, Saturday 5pm—11pm, closed Sunday
Tube Station: Leicester Square or Covent Garden

t's not just the name that's a giveaway. You know you've entered a shrine to the Gamay grape the moment you enter this wine bar. You have to squeeze past giant placards of different grape varieties just to get in. There are wine labels stuck to the lampshades and wine crates glued to the bar. Bizarrely, there are also hundreds of beer tankards dangling from the ceiling, along with dozens of ties belonging to denizens of the members-only restaurant in the basement next door.

"The place is of course older than I am," smiles Pascal Perry, the grey-haired, flush-cheeked manager installed behind the bar for over 30 years. Perry claims this was the first French wine bar in London. It opened in the 1960s as Winkles, but became "really French" in the '70s when Perry's predecessor Joel took over. It was Joel who started the tradition of confiscating customers' ties when they loosened up after a few drinks.

"Everything in this establishment is French except two things – my customers and my music," says Perry. He has a penchant for rock and blues, thankfully played at low volume. The Arsenal football merchandise doesn't look terribly French either, but there's no mistaking the provenance of the staff, whose accents are as creamy as ripe camembert. They know all the regulars (including many of their expat compatriots) by name.

Like the lived-in decor – a clutter of Gallic knick-knacks – the short menu never changes. It's rustic fare: a couple of plats du jour, rillettes, boeuf bourguignon, Toulouse sausages and a suitably stinky cheeseboard. The exclusively French wine list includes every Beaujolais appellation. Most are reasonably priced, but be prepared to take the rough with the smooth. Inevitably, it gets rammed when the Beaujolais Nouveau is released on the third Thursday of November. A special game-based lunch is served in the members' club, but gets booked up months in advance. To join the club, you must be recommended by a member or put in plenty of drinking hours at the bar.

Miraculously, the tourists swarming the West End always bypass this hideaway. Dark, cosy, occasionally loud, and consistently welcoming, Le Beaujolais warms the heart on a chilly winter's evening. Just a few doors down from The Ivy, it couldn't be less pretentious.

NEARBY
Rooftop
2 Spring Gardens, Trafalgar Square, SW1A 2TS
trafalgarstjames.com/the-rooftop
A summer sanctuary from the West End hordes, the rooftop bar at the Trafalgar Hotel has sensational city views, almost eye level with Nelson's Column and the London Eye.

UPSTAIRS AT RULES

Rules worth following

35 Maiden Lane, Covent Garden, WC2E 7LB
020 7836 5314
www.rules.co.uk
Monday–Saturday 12pm–11.30pm, Sunday 12pm–10.30pm
Tube station: Covent Garden or Charing Cross

"I hate rules", my drinking companion opined. But he looked extremely pleased with himself as he drained his Screaming Viking. Upstairs at Rules is my idea of the perfect cocktail bar. Hidden above London's oldest restaurant (est. 1798), this sumptuous hideaway was once a private dining room, where Edward VII canoodled with his paramour, Lillie Langtry. It's still a great venue for a clandestine date. Never advertised and rarely crowded, it's like having access to a gentlemen's club, without the fusty chauvinism or complicated door policy. All royal portraits, antlers and wood panelling, it's the kind of place where you can bring your lover, your mother or your boss.

Another great thing about this quintessentially British institution is the American-style service. Reserve a stool at the bar so you can get an eyeful of Bostonian bartender Brian Silva in action. Formerly at The Connaught and Scott's, Brian frowns on fruity flourishes and fancy garnishes (apart from the odd infusion of violet or rose petal). He serves classic cocktails inspired by the 1930s that feature his collection of rare spirits, including 42 vermouths. Most are stirred, not shaken. Brian will happily whip up a bespoke cocktail, based on your favourite tipple. But he has some special creations of his own, as dry as the wit who named them: perhaps Chorus Girl No 5, le Blonde, or my current favourite, Swedish Diplomat (Venezuelan Diplomatico rum, Swedish punch, and a squeeze of lime poured around a crystal ball of solid ice that melts ever so slowly, allowing the punchy spice to subtly infuse the drink).

Rules doesn't do music, beer, coffee or tea. But it does serve divine bar snacks as well as complimentary caramelised and curried nuts.

After his second Screaming Viking, my companion became fixated with the swirly scarlet and gold carpet. I was more intent on finding the fox hidden in the hunting frieze (salvaged from The Savoy during a recent makeover). Owner John Mayhew had himself, his dogs and his 1935 Rolls Royce "Bubbles" painted into the scene, which could just as well be Lartington, Mayhew's country estate. On shoot days, you must try the Buckshot Bullshot, Brian's twist on a Bloody Mary made with a shot of beef consommé.

Brian is usually on duty Tuesday to Saturday. Take my advice and treat yourself to a cocktail in his company on a dreary midweek afternoon. Just the sight of that gold "Reserved" sign on the gleaming bar is guaranteed to lift your spirits.

POETRY CAFÉ

Well versed

22 Betterton Street, Covent Garden, WC2H 9BX
020 7420 9887
www.poetrysociety.org.uk/poetry-cafe
Monday—Saturday 11am—11pm
Tube station: Covent Garden or Holborn

There's nothing glamorous or trendy about the Poetry Café, housed in the same building as The Poetry Society, founded in 1909 to promote the study and enjoyment of British verse. Unlike so many arts or academic institutions, it's neither self-important nor inaccessible. Like the brilliant "Poems on the Underground" initiative, the Poetry Café introduces a moment of quiet contemplation into the clutter and clamour of everyday life in London.

A haven from the West End hubbub in the backstreets of Covent Garden, the narrow, sparely furnished café is rarely busy during the day. There's usually the odd writer scrawling into a journal, poring over the small library of literary reviews and second-hand poetry volumes, or simply lost in thought. The staff will leave you in peace and let you linger as long as you like. The vegetarian food is pretty good, too. The daily menu includes mezze-style plates, a daily soup and stew, lots of yummy cakes and plenty of vegan and gluten free options. If you wish to drown your sorrows, the bar serves a whiskey called "Writers' Tears".

In the evenings, things liven up as the focus shifts to the poetry readings that take place in the basement. The atmosphere is intimate, supportive and sociable. There are events nearly every night (except Sundays), including regular open mic nights, book launches, and occasionally live music or screenings to accompany the verse. There's no need to book tickets in advance, but it's worth checking what's on before you go (www.poetrysociety.org.uk/events/calendar).

NEARBY
Amphitheatre Restaurant
Royal Opera House, Bow Street, WC2B
020 7212 9254
www.roh.org.uk
In the evenings, this swish restaurant on the top floor of the Royal Opera House is only open to ticket holders. At lunchtime, anyone can enjoy British comfort food with marvellous views of Covent Garden's market and across the rooftops to Nelson's Column. It's especially lovely on summer afternoons, when tables are set on a secret terrace.

MUSEUM OF COMEDY

Comedy heaven

The Undercroft, St George's Church, Bloomsbury Way, WC1A 2SR
020 7534 1744
www.museumofcomedy.com
foh@museumofcomedy.com
Daily 12pm/1pm—10pm; check website as hours may vary depending on performances
Tube station: Tottenham Court Road or Holborn

The Museum of Comedy is less like a museum and more like a church cellar bar where comedy is the religion. Sip plonk in pews from the set of *Father Ted*, *Rev.* or *The Vicar of Dibley* and pray to the comedy idolatry around you: Tommy Cooper's magic props, Steptoe and Son's stuffed bear, Lilly Savage's wigs, Little Titch's big shoes and Bill Bailey's six-neck guitar. Or down your beer on the banquette where Spike Milligan wrote the Goon Show and spin one of over 1,400 comedy LPs on Spike's very own turntable.

And all this because of a pre-nup clause. The extraordinary collection of memorabilia from the laughter biz was amassed by comedy impresario and impressive comedy prop-maker Martin Witts. But if he wanted to walk his fiancée Lesley down the aisle, first he had to clear out the

Photo by Steve Ullathorne

comedy clutter which not only filled his house but several garages, three hen sheds and a narrowboat on the river Ouse.

When Martin first started to move it all into the Bloomsbury church basement, it was a bit cramped as it was still home to 840 coffins, one of which was discovered to contain genuine funny bones – those of Joseph Shepherd Munden, who had entertained 19th-century London audiences with facial contortions and drunk impersonations. You'll find his medal awarded for "bile and humour" in one of the displays. Not all the comedians here are dead – you can find real live ones trying not to die on stage next door in the Comedy Crypt. Often they are big name stand-ups pre-testing their material on smaller audiences before they set off on grand tours. And if you think your bones might also be funny, the undercroft also hosts courses and workshops in comedy. The courses and stage acts are ticketed, but Monday nights there's free comedy in the bar from 7pm. Sometimes the same deal happens unofficially – apparently Paul Merton and Suki Webster can prop up the post-show bar 'til all hours. But crammed as the museum is, marriage doesn't seem to have tamed Martin's hoarding habit. He's just acquired Fred "the cabbie who won Mastermind" Housego's comedy radio show record collection. And what with all the comedians who keep dying and leaving him stuff, the museum is already spilling out into its sister venue at the Leicester Square Theatre – only a short funny walk away.

CAMERA MUSEUM COFFEE SHOP

Click bait

44 Museum Street, Bloomsbury, WC1A 1LY
020 7242 8681
www.cameramuseum.uk
cameramuseumuk@gmail.com
Monday–Friday 11am–7pm, Saturday 12pm–7pm
Tube station: Tottenham Court Road or Holborn

The backstreets opposite the British Museum aren't just crawling with tourists. Professional photographers scour the area's camera shops for specialist gear. Beside the cabinets of second-hand Leicas, Nikons and Hasselblads on sale at Aperture is this tiny café, run by amateur snapper and chilli lover Adrian Tang.

His quirky coffee shop has been around since 1999 in various guises. First it was Tang, then The Museum Café, "but tourists kept coming in

asking where the entrance to the British Museum was." Tang tried his hand at poetry nights until eventually he hit upon the idea of adding a camera shop to boost business. It worked so well, he added a little museum in the basement rooms – with a timeline of camera equipment stretching across the walls in a chronological grid – starting in the 1800s and disappearing into the digital age. It's free to enter, and you get to play with beautiful old Super-8 movie cameras and whirr-click a vintage Hasselblad.

Upstairs in the coffee shop, many of the regulars are camera buffs. Others come for Tang's excellent classical and jazz collection, tip-tapping away on their laptops and taking advantage of the free wifi. They are served hot drinks, fresh-pressed juices, toasted paninis, home-made soups, cakes and cookies, with just a trace of the previous Chinese menu in the form of a dim sum platter and king prawn soup.

Tang encourages donations – his aim is to find one of every model of camera – but with 40,000 in existence and counting, he might end up having to tunnel under the British Museum.

NEARBY
London Review Cake Shop

14 Bury Place, Bloomsbury, WC1A 2JL
020 7269 9030
www.lrbshop.co.uk/cakeshop

Wander through the history section of this inspiring bookshop and you'll find an elegant café that serves fabulous Monmouth coffee, Jing teas, and all sorts of irresistible treats (the blueberry cake is heavenly). Savoury dishes – freshly prepared salads, sandwiches and small plates – are just as good. Most customers are quietly engrossed in the books and periodicals scattered about the communal tables.

ARCHITECTURAL ASSOCIATION DINING ROOM

Chic and cheap

36 Bedford Square, Bloomsbury, WC1B 3ES
020 7887 4091
www.aaschool.ac.uk
Dining room: Monday—Friday 12:15pm—2:30pm
Bar: Monday—Friday 9:15am—9pm, Saturday 11am—5pm
Tube station: Tottenham Court Road or Goode Street

O f all Bloomsbury's beautiful garden squares, Bedford Square is perhaps the loveliest. The Architectural Association's School of Architecture, which occupies a whole sweep of Georgian splendour on the western side of the square, is surely one of the most elegant campuses anywhere in London. Founded in 1847, the AA opened as a day school in 1901 and moved to Bedford Square in 1917.

Faculties are split between ten townhouses, but No. 36 is the school's public face. Students' work in progress is displayed around the building. The elegant ground-floor parlour has been converted into an exhibition space, which hosts architecture, interior design and photography. The work is eclectic but always fascinating: Gio Ponti chairs, temporary structures fashioned by homeless Americans, the unbuilt architecture of London.

Exhibitions often spill over into the first floor bar. With cheap beers and bay windows overlooking Bedford Square, it's the kind of place where you could easily lose a whole afternoon. Hidden at the back is a terrace where you can bunk off work and nobody will find you.

Although it's open to the public, you'd never know there was a dining room in the basement. There's nothing to alert visitors to its existence. The big, bright room is characteristically well designed (by one of the AA's tutors), with a black floor, plain wooden chairs and large tables in block colours. Lunch, prepared by long-standing chef Pascal Babeau, is laid out on a mosaic counter. The self-service salad selection raises the bar: there's no limp lettuce or soggy sweetcorn here; it's all Asian noodles, spinach, beetroot and grapefruit, and just grated coleslaw. There are two or three hot meals, which might be tomato, olive and mozzarella quiche, mushroom casserole or beef curry served with rice. It's unbeatable value: hefty portions of home cooking at supermarket prices in stylish surroundings. Go early to avoid disappointment: after 2.15pm, they only serve gourmet sandwiches (try the Parma ham, parmesan, sun blush tomatoes and salad) and pizzas.

NEARBY
Bradley's Spanish Bar
42–44 Hanway Street, Fitzrovia, W1T 1UP
020 7636 0359
www.bradleysspanishbar.com
Among the many late-night Spanish dives on Hanway Street, Bradley's is easily the most appealing. This cramped, chaotic, delightful bar has one of the last surviving vinyl jukeboxes in London. The rotating collection of singles spans everything from The Supremes to The White Stripes.

POSTCARD TEAS

Just add water

9 Dering Street, Mayfair, W1S 1AG
020 7629 3654
www.postcardteas.com
info@postcardteas.com
Monday–Friday 10.30am–6.30pm, Saturday 11am–6.30pm
Tube station: Bond Street or Oxford Circus

Britain's colonial past has created a nation of tea lovers. Whereas most people would settle for PG Tips, Timothy d'Offay's pursuit of the perfect cuppa has taken him all over India and the Far East. At Postcard Teas, connoisseurs can sample his signature blends and single-estate teas from India, Sri Lanka, China, Japan, Taiwan, Korea and Vietnam.

The loose-leaf tea is sold in elegant caddies decorated with vintage postcards from Tim's personal collection. Alternatively, vacuum-packed pouches of chai and oolong can be posted directly to fellow tea fanatics worldwide from the shop's own red letterbox. A postmark shows the tea's provenance, including the estate and region where it was produced. It's not your typical mail order – but this is not your typical teashop.

Tea was first sold here 200 years ago when this was a grocery store;

the original 18th-century frontage is intact. The spare interior offers a welcome respite from the bling of Bond Street. A pared-down Japanese aesthetic and barely audible classical music create a cocoon of calm, even when it's busy. "The shop was born out of the frustration of buying expensive tea from food halls, but not being able to taste or even smell it," says Tim, as he brews me a cup of Master Matsumoto's "Supernatural" tea – it won't give you super-powers, but it's absolutely pesticide and fertiliser free. The shop also stocks delightful tea paraphernalia such as patchwork tea cosies from India and tin caddies hand-made in Kyoto.

All the teas can be tried at the communal tasting table, each one served in a different cup, beaker or saucer that reflects its roots. The rarest teas are made from ancient plants using ancestral techniques. Master Luo has had the honour of making green tea from the 18 bushes reserved for the Chinese President since the 18th century. The Liu family make Pu-erh tea from trees that dates back to the time of Gengis Khan.

Tasting notes such as "a sweet soft sencha with lots of umami", "a mild grassy green tea with a citrus finish", might sound pretentious; Postcard Teas is aimed at purists, yet it's surprisingly accessible. Come alone and savour a delicate cup of tea and a delicious moment of solitude – a restorative ritual worth repeating every day. But remember: there's no toilet, so don't drink too much.

L'ATELIER DES CHEFS

Making a meal of it

19 Wigmore Street, Marylebone, W1U 1PH
020 7499 6580
www.atelierdeschefs.co.uk
Monday–Saturday 10am–7pm ; check website for details as class times vary
Tube station: Oxford Circus or Bond Street

This culinary school provides instant gratification: you can eat what you've cooked as soon as your dishes are ready. There are classes for all abilities: you can squeeze a half-hour session into your lunch break, perfect pasta making in two hours, or take a four-hour master-class in Indian cuisine. I chose a ninety-minute Cook and Dine evening class, with a menu apparently lifted from an Islington gastro-pub: mushroom velouté, rump steak with truffled crushed potatoes and creamy Savoy cabbage, followed by sticky toffee pudding with crème anglaise.

Eight of us had signed up. My fellow students were a statuesque French woman who had come to master the art of sticky toffee pudding ("I adore British food," she sighed), two young editors from Bloomsbury ("We publish Heston and Hugh so we get to try out all their recipes"), a teenage trainee chef from Leeds with her mum ("This is way more hands-on than catering college – all we ever make is biscuits"), and a couple of law students from Canada (who seemed more interested in eating each other than our three-course dinner).

Donning plastic aprons, we rolled up our sleeves and gathered round chef Louis Solley's spotless stove. Solley, a puckish character with dazzling knife skills and a quick wit, is a natural teacher. He makes everything look simple and puts everyone at ease. "Normally I'm locked in a basement kitchen with nobody to talk to, so I like to give the customers a good grilling."

We started with dessert, the trickiest dish on tonight's menu. We beat the sugar, and butter by hand, instead of in a food processor, avoiding wrist strain as we took turns blending the mixture to golden putty. Tasks are divided to save time, but we all get our hands dirty.

Louis had pre-prepared a wild mushroom stock for the soup. He showed us how to finely dice shallots, although it took me five times longer than him. I learned how to smash raw garlic and salt into a smooth paste, and discovered that you should only slice parsley once or it will go bitter. The men relish the job of searing the steaks over a smoking pan. The table is laid while we're clumsily piping goat's cheese and crème fraiche onto warm croutons.

We ate each course together, oohing and aahing over the results. Louis tells us his cholesterol is 8.5; after devouring three courses in which butter and cream are the star ingredients, I can see why. But every bite was worth it.

PAUL ROTHE & SON

Tea and sympathy

35 Marylebone Lane, Marylebone, W1U 2NN
020 7935 6783
Monday–Friday 8am–5pm, Saturday 11.30am–5pm
Tube station: Marble Arch or Bond Street

There's something utterly irresistible about a café with a large sign outside that says: HOT SOUP. At this charming time warp, the soup in question never fails to delight, whether it's creamy leek and potato or spicy Thai chicken. Served in pretty vintage bowls with a crusty buttered roll, the potage is as comforting as the kindly staff, invariably wearing white coats and a smile.

This quaint café, which doubles as a delicatessen, is as much about the people as the superlative produce. Dating back to 1900, it's been in the Rothe family for four generations – ever since the current owner's German grandfather arrived in London on a coal barge. "At the time, it was one of only three delicatessens in London. People would come from all over town for their rye loaves," says Paul Rothe, who has been installed behind the sandwich bar since 1969.

Devoted regulars still come from far and wide for the Ukrainian rye bread. Despite the ongoing chi-chification of Marylebone, Paul Rothe & Son has preserved the old-fashioned charm of the village grocer. Wood-clad walls are lined with traditional treats evocative of children's parties and family picnics – chutneys and pickles, preserves and marmalades, lemon curd, English mustard, peppermint humbugs and Highland fudge.

The eat-in or take-away menu is also a smorgasbord of comfort food for the terminally nostalgic: marmite and cucumber sandwiches, salt beef, mustard and dill pickle baps, a mug of Bovril, a caramel slice. A few exotic items do feature, notably the Austrian liptauer (cream cheese with paprika, chives and capers) and kummelkase (stilton, caraway seeds and cream cheese) sandwiches.

Order at the counter and take a seat in one of the Formica booths with folding leatherette seats. There's great pleasure to be had from eavesdropping on Rothe & Son's conversations with their customers, who range from despatch riders to besuited businessmen.

"Have we tempted you with anything else?" Rothe asks an elegant octogenarian stocking up on cranberry and pistachio cake.

"I had a different combination altogether today – I'm trying to catch you out," teases one regular, as she pays for her Scotch egg and liver sausage sandwich.

"No tomatoes, please," says a glamorous American, with a wave of her manicured hand.

"But they're very good for you."

"I don't like them."

All in all, a most civilised way to spend an afternoon.

Shops with secret refreshments

If you're out to shop, then drop in on one of these stores, where you will find comestibles to keep you sustained as you browse the consumables.

PAPER DRESS VINTAGE

352a Mare Street, Hackney E8 1HR
020 8510 0520 – paperdressvintage.co.uk
Amazing retro clothes shop and cultural hub, with a café/bar events space licensed 'til 3am on Saturdays. You might find Go-Go girls shopping for knee-high boots in store or indeed dancing in the shop window.

NOVELTY AUTOMATION

1a Princeton Street, Holborn WC1R 4AX
novelty-automation.com
On the first Thursday of the month, you can drink and play at this arcade full of hilarious retro end-of-the-pier games machines, created by cartoonist-engineer Tim Hunkin. The "Instant Weight Loss" machine will produce a meal for you that might leave you slightly wanting. Stem your hunger entirely by playing "Pet or Meat", where the fate of an innocent bleating lamb is decided by the spin of a roulette wheel.

LUTYENS & RUBINSTEIN

21 Kensington Park Road, Notting Hill, W11 2EU
020 7229 1010 – www.lutyensrubinstein.co.uk
This supremely stylish bookstore, run by literary agents, has an espresso machine in the basement so you can drink coffee in hand-made china cups decorated with the first lines of famous novels, while browsing the hand-picked book collection.

BRILL

27 Exmouth Market, Clerkenwell, EC1R 4QL
020 7833 9757 – exmouth.london/brill
Bagels, cappuccinos, and a brilliant selection of vinyl and CDs make this the perfect little local record store. They've even got a secret

garden. Fridays are late-running Brill nights, with good music and cheap booze until 11pm.

SHIP OF ADVENTURES

138 Kingsland High Street, Hackney E8 2NS
020 3327 1777 – www.hackneypirates.org

Everything is ship shape in the Hackney Pirate's children's bookshop and café, with hidden tunnel and magic telephone. A great place to take the kids, but also often child-free during school hours. Buy the delicious freshly made sandwiches, salads and yummy cakes and support the excellent work of this children's literacy charity.

ASSAL

14 Connaught Street, Marble Arch, W2 2AF
020 7706 2905

This Persian patisserie has a couple of tables on the pavement outside where you can have your pistachio and pine-nut cookies or sublime saffron ice cream with mint tea or cardamom coffee.

MARKUS COFFEE CO LTD

13 Connaught Street, Marble Arch, W2 2AY
020 7262 4630 – www.markuscoffee.com

This delightful period piece has been supplying coffee to London's top restaurants since 1957. Thirty-four varieties of beans (including their secret Regent and Negresco blend) are roasted on the premises daily, using the same Probata machine as when the shop opened. The aroma is irresistible.

NEWENS

288 Kew Road, Richmond TW9 3DU
0208 940 2752 – www.theoriginalmaidsofhonour.co.uk

Also known as "The Original Maids of Honour", this bakery specialises in a melt-in-the-mouth English custard tart that was apparently a favourite of Henry VIII. His tarts are amazing, but so are all the pies, pastries and sweatmeats, cooked up in a vintage kitchen and served in the adjoining tearooms. If you want to beat the crowds at Kew, stay over in their vintage B&B upstairs.

WALLACE COLLECTION COURTYARD

Dressed in salmon pink

Hertford House, Manchester Square, Marylebone, W1U 3BN
0207 563 9505
www.thewallacerestaurant.com
reservations@thewallacerestaurant.com
Sunday–Thursday 10am–5pm (last orders 4.30pm), Friday–Saturday 10am–11pm (last orders 9.30pm)
Tube station: Bond Street or Baker Street

The Victoria & Albert was the world's first museum with a public restaurant, offering first-, second- and third-class menus depending on the visitor's social status. The Wallace Collection's restaurant seems to be designed squarely with the upper crust in mind. In a soaring, salmon-pink courtyard, this elegant brasserie is hidden inside a stately home stuffed with old masters, suits of armour, and all manner of trifles and trinkets.

Hertford House, a huge pile just behind Oxford Street, belonged to the Marquesses of Hertford, a succession of reprobates with refined tastes who amassed a vast collection of 18th- and 19th-century art and antiques. The 25 rooms are decked out as they would have been while the aristocrats were in residence: with clashing wallpaper, lashings of porcelain, and old masters by Rembrandt, Rubens, Velázquez and Van Dyck. When British Prime Minister Benjamin Disraeli signed the visitors' book in 1878, he described it as a "palace of genius, fancy and taste". Bequeathed to the nation in 1897, the collection also includes one of the largest arrays of armour in the UK (visitors can try on chain mail for size in the Conservation Gallery). One room is filled with furniture that belonged to Queen Marie-Antoinette of France.

The Wallace Restaurant is rather like being transported to the court of Versailles – or, at least, a Parisian arcade. It's like a miniature (but much more intimate) version of the Great Court at the British Museum.

In the winter they light the place with fairy lights and candles and it's magical. The menu consists of serve small and large seasonal plates of Anglo-French dishes. The afternoon high teas are very popular. Breakfast is a great time to visit, when the place is quiet and you can feast on eggs Benedict in perfect peace. Or go for a romantic rendez-vous on Friday or Saturday evening, when the restaurant stays open for dinner after the museum has closed. The sumptuous setting invites extravagance: it's the kind of place where you can't resist ordering a glass of champagne. Postprandial canoodling is pretty much guaranteed.

RIBA CAFÉ

Building builders' cafe

66 Portland Place, Fitzrovia, W1B 1AD
020 7631 0467
www.architecture.com
Monday—Friday 8am—5pm, Saturday 10am—5pm
Tube station: Great Portland Street or Oxford Circus

I've often wandered past the magnificent embassies on Portland Place and wondered what lavish banquets are underway within their soaring halls. Edward Davenport turned this fantasy into a lucrative business, renting out 33 Portland Place for film shoots and orgies – until his conviction for fraud abruptly ended the party.

Those of us who aren't ambassadors, celebrities or sex kittens can get a taste of the Portland Place high life at RIBA, the Royal Institute of British Architects. Founded in 1834, RIBA's current headquarters opened a century later. The six-storey building faced in Portland stone is minimalist and effortlessly modern: there's no gilt, no patterned carpets, no imposing portraits on the walls. Massive bronze doors, decorated with a relief of London's riverside landmarks, lead to a grand marble and glass staircase.

There's a perfect geometry and harmony to the space. Carved reliefs depicting "man and his buildings through the ages" decorate the ceiling and window piers. Sadly, the first-floor restaurant is no more, but the ground-floor café serves food and drinks all day and you can take them upstairs to the grand surrounds of the gallery room. Or out onto the beautifully landscaped roof terrace with living walls – perfect for a clandestine date or a quiet read. When I visited recently on a Thursday afternoon, I had the whole place to myself.

Afterwards, browse the architecture library on the third floor, which holds over 150,000 books, 1.5 million photographs, and even a fragment of Sir Christopher Wren's coffin.

INDIAN YMCA

Curry favour

41 Fitzroy Square, Fitzrovia, W1T 6AQ
020 7387 0411
www.indianymca.org
enquiries@indianymca.org
Monday–Friday 7.30am–9.15am, 12pm–2pm, 6.30pm–8.30pm,
weekends and bank holidays 8am–9.30am, 12.00pm–1.30pm, 6.30pm–8.30pm
Tube station: Warren Street, Euston Square or Goodge Street

Youth hostels aren't places I'd normally associate with good food. If YMCA brings to mind Village People rather than hot dinners, you'll be surprised by this odd little anachronism in Fitzrovia. Founded in 1920 to provide affordable accommodation for Indian students in London, the Indian YMCA has survived several incarnations. These premises on Fitzroy Square were officially opened by the High Commissioner of India in 1953. Even Ghandi and Nehru came to give their blessings. In 1962, this became London's first mixed-sex youth hostel, a surprisingly racy move for such a conservative establishment.

In all other respects, the atmosphere at this charming time warp is comfortingly institutional. In the cafeteria, impoverished students hunch over heaped plates of super-cheap curries alongside thrifty academics, office workers and Indian expats pining for a taste of home. Attentive staff in white jackets and hats chitchat with the regulars in Hindi. The room bears all the hallmarks of a canteen in any subcontinental backwater, right down to the Formica tables, beige curtains, neon lighting, and a washbasin for traditionalists who prefer to eschew cutlery.

Fine dining, this ain't. It's self-service. Vats of mutton, fish, and chicken curry look fairly indistinguishable, but they're all tasty and freshly made. A mound of pilau rice, hot spiced cabbage and lentil curry, onion bhajis, and saucers of chutney and raita will set you back less than a tenner. Mango lassi and watermelon juice are on offer, and there are jugs of tap water on every table. Ghee is used sparingly, so the food doesn't leave a greasy aftertaste despite the giant servings.

The cafeteria is open for just an hour or two each mealtime. There's a lunch-break rush around 1pm, so go earlier or later to be sure of a seat. It's not a place for a leisurely meal, but it's ideal for lunch on a busy day, or a budget dinner with a gang of friends. And if you stay in one of their bargain hostel rooms, breakfast and dinner are included.

NEARBY
Archipelago
53 Cleveland Street, Fitzrovia. W1T 4JJ
020 7637 9611
www.archipelago-restaurant.co.uk
Everything about this restaurant is self-consciously quirky: the bill arrives in a treasure chest, and there are garlic locusts, chocolate-covered scorpions, kangaroo and crocodile on the menu. Beware of ordering "a visit from the doctor" …

PAOLINA'S THAI CAFÉ

Cheap dates and hot noodles

181 King's Cross Road, King's Cross, WC1X 9BZ
020 7278 8176
www.paolinathaicuisine.co.uk
paolinathaicuisine@gmail.com
Monday–Friday 12pm–3pm and 6pm–10pm, Saturday 6pm–10pm;
closed Sunday
Tube station: King's Cross

I lived around the corner from this place for a couple of years, and I must have eaten here at least 50 times. Yet my next-door neighbour, who had lived in the area for a decade, had never heard of it. Perhaps that's because Paolina sure isn't a looker at first glance. Hurrying along this dingy stretch of King's Cross Road, it would be easy to overlook the faded yellow shop front with its wobbly hand-drawn sign. Even if you peered through the doorway, you probably wouldn't be tempted inside: the cluttered kitchen at the front looks like an unsavoury takeaway. But venture in and you'll be pleasantly surprised.

Squeeze past the smiling chefs, sweating over steaming vats of noodles, and you'll discover a tiny dining room hidden at the rear. (Tinier still is the WC – surely the smallest in London?) Wood-panelled, with no windows, the restaurant is cosiest on frosty evenings. The same plastic flowers, Formica tables and portraits of Thai royalty appear to have been there since the 1970s, although in fact this Thai café opened in 1996. Prior to that, it was an Italian caff run by the eponymous Paolina. The new owners didn't bother to change the name as they couldn't afford a new sign.

Punters are packed in tight but there's always a buzzy, easy camaraderie. Most diners are regulars who come for the pitch-perfect pad Thai and fantastically friendly service. Paolina's is family-run and the food tastes like home cooking. Starters rely heavily on the deep fryer, so I usually stick to hot and sour soups such as tom kha gai (chicken, coconut milk, lemongrass and lime leaves) or red-hot salads such as som tum (papaya with chillies, ground peanuts and dried shrimp). Curries won't blow your brains out as they do in many Thai restaurants, which is good news for chilli lightweights like me. But it's the stir-fried dishes that stand out – particularly that pad Thai.

This is one of those rare London restaurants where you can have a fine supper for a tenner. You can bring your own booze; the corkage charge is £2. Call me a cheap date, but in my book Paolina's is perfect for a romantic rendezvous. The cheerful welcome was one of the things I missed most when I moved out of King's Cross, but it's still waiting for me every time I go back.

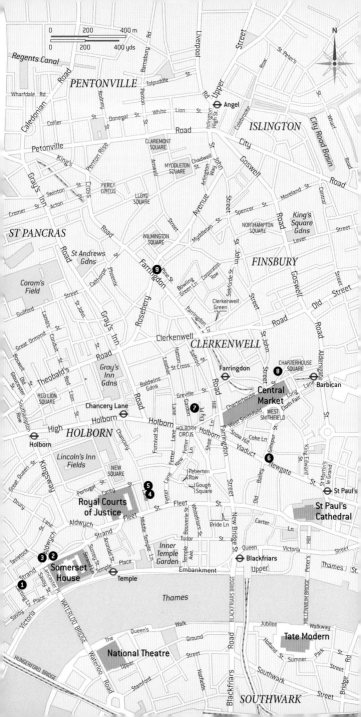

Temple to Angel

KNIGHT'S BAR

Grand Master

Simpson's-in-the-Strand, 100 Strand, Aldwych, WC2R OEW
020 7420 2111
www.simpsonsinthestrand.co.uk
savoy@fairmont.com
Monday—Saturday 11:30am—11pm, Sunday 11:30am—8pm
Tube station: Temple, Charing Cross or Embankment

S impson's-in-the-Strand is one of those venerable London institutions that regulars prefer to keep to themselves. Fashionable haunts such as The Wolseley and The Delaunay may offer a pseudo slice of old-world refinement, but Simpson's is the real deal. While those young pretenders trade in Viennese exoticism, Simpson's is resolutely British. Back in 1862, Master Cook Thomas Davey insisted that everything served in the restaurant must be British (he even replaced the "menu" with a "bill of fare"). This tradition continues, with native delights such as steak and kidney pudding, and the WWII vegetarian option, Lord Woolton pie, invented at the Savoy and recommended to housewives by the Ministry of Food. The *pièce de résistance* is the roast rib of Scottish beef, carved at table by liveried waiters from silver-domed trolleys. This practice began during Simpson's original incarnation as a chess club: the meat was wheeled out to avoid disturbing the players' concentration. The

original booths, or divans, that line one wall of the glorious Edwardian dining room were reserved for chess players. Chess matches were played against other coffee houses, with top-hatted runners carrying news of each move between venues. A chess set is still available, but nowadays diners discussing "fish" are more likely to be talking about the Dover sole than a feeble opponent.

The aroma of roast beef follows you upstairs to the Knight's Bar, an Art Deco hideaway overlooking The Strand. With its gold and black chequerboard bar, squishy armchairs and velvet settees burnished by many distinguished bottoms, the bar looks as though it's been here for decades; in fact it opened in 1999. Rarely crowded, it's perfect for pre- or post-theatre drinks without the usual West End crush. The drinks list includes a fine selection of English "champagnes" and all the classics, as well as superlative signature cocktails inspired by the kitchen gardens, orchards and allotments of Britain. The bar menu even features a snack version of their roast beef and Yorkshire pudding.

You can entertain yourself by trying to identify the black and white portraits of famous movie stars, statesmen, boxers and tennis players lining the walls. Many are inscribed to Mr Heck, General Manager of Simpson's from 1919 to 1959. Past patrons include Vincent Van Gogh, Charles Dickens and Charlie Chaplin. George Bernard Shaw was among the diners forced to take shelter in the wine cellar during an air raid in 1917. Shaw left a thank-you note inscribed on the kitchen wall, which survives today.

INDIA CLUB

A colonial curry house

143 Strand, Aldwych, WC2R 1JA
020 7836 4880
www.strand-continental.co.uk
strandcontinentalhotel@gmail.com
Daily 12pm–2.30pm, 6pm–10.50pm
Tube station: Temple, Covent Garden, Embankment or Charing Cross

V.K. Krishna Menon, independent India's first High Commissioner in Britain, allegedly drank 50 cups of tea every day. When Menon moved into India House on Aldwych in 1947, he set up the India Club (across the road on the Strand) as somewhere for expats and diplomats to chew the fat over chai after office hours. With founding members including Jawaharlal Nehru and Lady Edwina Mountbatten, the India Club was a hotbed of political activity – and maybe more, as the two allegedly had an affair.

The India Club has survived intact, hidden up a flight of grubby linoleum stairs in the Strand Continental Hotel (don't be fooled by the name – it's a hostel with bargain bedrooms overlooking the Thames). With its cracked leather armchairs, the lounge has been preserved in aspic. It has definitely seen better days. But there's a certain allure to a bar that makes no concession to coolness, though they have replaced the

Ravi Shankar cassettes with soul and disco funk. It's still occasionally frequented by the octogenarian members of the Calcutta Rowing Club.

Most patrons pick up some Cobra beers or bring their own booze (there's no corkage charge) and head upstairs to the delightful dining room. With its dark wooden chairs with padded leather seats and portraits of Gandhi, it has the feel of a refectory in a provincial Indian university; in fact, most customers are students and professors from King's College and the LSE, or barristers from the Inns of Court nearby.

In 1957, Menon delivered an eight-hour speech defending India's stand on Kashmir – the longest oration ever delivered at the United Nations. The laconic waiters are less verbose. Dressed in white jackets, they look as though they've been there forever – and most have indeed been around for decades. Gyanaprakasam Joseph, head waiter for 37 years, was such an institution that his obituary was published in *The Guardian*.

The menu still reflects Menon's roots in Kerala, featuring many southern Indian dishes such as *sambar* (tamarind-infused lentil curry), *masala dosa* (crispy pancakes with coconut chutney) and *panipuri* (crisp hollow puffs to crack open and fill with with tamarind water & spicy chickpeas). It's simple home-style cooking, refreshingly free from the lashings of ghee used in so many British curry houses. The lamb *bhuna* and *mughlai* chicken are very good, but only the brave should try the whole chilli *bhajas*. The set menus (vegetarian, meat, or prawn) are a steal.

CELLARDOOR

Louche loos

Zero Aldwych, Covent Garden, WC2E 7DN
020 7240 8848
www.cellardoor.biz
angel@cellardoor.biz
Monday–Friday 4pm–1am, Saturday 6pm–1am, Sunday 7pm –1am
Tube sation: Temple, Covent Garden or Charing Cross

"I ran May Balls at University, went to the occasional lecture and wrote the odd essay. Thirty years later, I'm still doing exactly the same thing," says Paul Kohler, who clearly relishes his double life as a club owner and law professor.

Kohler's underground bar takes its WC postcode very literally. Formerly the Wellington Street Gents, this public convenience was allegedly frequented by celebrity cruisers Oscar Wilde, John Gielgud and John Hurt. "I'd walked past this disused public toilet every day for years – a prime space in the heart of London – and just thought: why not?" Kohler recalls.

Kohler persuaded Westminster Council to grant him a late licence as long as he staged live entertainment. Since the tiny space only holds 60 people, Kohler plumped for cabaret, which comes from the Dutch word "*camberete*", meaning "small room". Every night is different, from burlesque shows to drag DJs, saucy comedy acts to singers belting out tunes from the Weimar Republic. Many unsigned acts can claim to have made their West End debut here. Unlike the surrounding theatres, there's no cover charge and even the popcorn is free. On Sunday afternoons they hold Kinema & Kocktails, with a silent short screening at 4.30pm and a main movie at 5pm.

The street-level entrance looks like a futuristic version of the Paris Metro. Downstairs, walls of angled mirrors and coloured spotlights create the illusion of space. The minute stage, surrounded by scarlet and black banquettes, is concealed by velvet drapes. They've even managed to squeeze in a piano and a dance floor. You have to edge past the performers to get to the toilets, which are designed to titillate. The transparent glass doors become opaque when you lock them. "It's great," says Kohler. "People never leave the loos in a mess when they know you can see inside."

Both glamorous and faintly sleazy, this is something of a pick-up joint. The text message jukebox is a clever icebreaker for courting couples. There always seem to be a few businessmen buying drinks for pretty young things. And this is probably the only place in London where you can do lines on the bar and nobody will bat an eyelid. They sell snuff in all manner of strange flavours from apricot to absinthe, champagne to Red Bull.

BARANIS

An underground court

115 Chancery Lane, Holborn, WC2A 1PP
www. baranis.co.uk
bookings@baranis.co.uk
Tuesday–Friday 4pm–late, Saturday 5pm–late
Tube station: Chancery Lane, Temple or Holborn

Down some steep steps in the depths of London's legal quarter, you'll find an unexpected slice of 1950s Côte d'Azur glam and the only indoor pétanque court in Britain. At Baranis (a play on Bar Anis, as in the

Photos by Carla Romero

French for aniseed) you can toss your boules all year round, even when the weather isn't quite Riviera style. Though the night my Anglo-Franco-Scots trio choose to drop in is during the hottest week of the longest British summer any of us have experienced – even the French contingent is a little piqued.

The cool cellar is a pleasant escape from the baking 35 degrees above. The bare brick walls are lined with shipshape tables and benches. We sit in an alcove below the halter-necked bosoms of a St Tropez bathing belle and order from a Provençal-inspired cocktail list. Our favourites are the thick floral French martini, the basil-topped "Green Candy" and the "Pomme Fanny", though the last one might just be that we like the name. If you have a penchant for aniseed, they have the biggest pastis and absinthe menu in London. We soak up the pre-match alcohol with some scrumptious Niçoise snacks – *panisses* (chunky chickpea chips) and *pissaladière* (pizza-style bread topped with caramelised onion and anchovies).

Our pétanque session has been booked well in advance – there's only one lane, so you need to swoop in ahead of the local legal eagles. This is the first time two of us have played properly, but we very quickly get into a highly competitive and slightly nationalistic ball game. Heavy metal thuds to the ground, bouncing ochre gravel in its wake. Despite an early Scots surge, England soon dominates, forcing a tactical Auld alliance. We attempt to disrupt with a Highland shot-put throw and a little French *je ne sais quoi*, but only succeed in knocking our oppressor's ball closer to the coche. With no measuring tape or attorney on hand, we settle close calls with the aid of a long USB cable. I'm not sure how this method would hold

up in court. When the thirteenth point is scored, it's typically disaster for Scotland. The Franco-Scots front have failed tragically to knock the cockney bird off her perch. Humph – and she thought Baranis rhymed with sarnies. For more on petanque, see page 158.

NEARBY
The Vulliamy Lounge ⑤
113 Chancery Lane, WC2A 1PL
www.113chancerylane.co.uk
0207 316 5580

The Law Society's restaurant, previously known as the Six Clerks or just 113 Chancery Lane, has been newly refurbished and is open to all. Serving British seasonal dishes, its new name is in honour of Lewis Vulliamy (1791-1871) who was one of the architects of the Law Society building. Inside you will also find four clocks made by his brother, Benjamin Lewis.

THE VIADUCT TAVERN

A jailhouse in a gin palace

126 Newgate Street, The City of London, EC1A 7AA
020 7600 1863
www.viaducttavern.co.uk
viaduct@fullers.co.uk
Monday–Friday 11am–11pm
Tube station: St Paul's
Rail station: City Thameslink

The Victorians were gluttons for punishment – capital crimes included impersonating an Egyptian, stealing an heiress, and poaching a rabbit; but they were also gluttons for gin. This 19th-century pub combines the two. The first public building in London equipped with electric lighting, the Viaduct Tavern is one of the city's last surviving gin palaces. These lavishly decorated boozers, where the upper classes mingled with low life, first appeared around 1830.

With its gold-edged mirrors and beaten copper ceiling, this pub is a typical example. The giant triptych represents the statues of Commerce, Agriculture, Science and Fine Arts on nearby Holborn Viaduct, which opened in 1869, the same year as the pub (look for the wound in Science's rump, pierced by a soldier's bayonet during celebrations to mark the end of the First World War). The landlady would dispense gin tokens from the

mahogany and etched-glass booth behind the bar. The pub still does a fine gin and tonic, with a choice of over ten gins.

However, the romantic interior doesn't prepare you for the horrors in the basement. The pub was built on the site of the Giltspur Comptor, a sheriff's office with a debtors' gaol affiliated to Newgate Prison. Little remains of this infamous prison, the city's main jail for almost five centuries. Originally located by a medieval gate in the Roman London Wall, it was demolished in 1902. The Central Criminal Courts now stand on the site.

If you ask nicely, the staff will show you five cells that survived the prison's closure, now used in part as beer cellars. Bitterly cold, damp and dark, the underground cells still look like the real deal. The ghost of a young prostitute supposedly haunts one cell, but visitors don't need to be psychic to sniff out the misery. Up to twenty criminals – men, women, children – and countless rats were crammed into each 12 by 8 feet cell. There was no toilet; one gaoler described the stench as "enough to turn the stomach of a horse." The only daylight was from a hole in the ceiling leading to street level, used by relatives or sympathetic passers-by to drop down scraps of food.

When I expressed horror at these conditions, the Polish waitress shrugged. "At least they wouldn't want to come back – now prison is like a hotel." Ironically, George Michael's *Freedom* was playing when we surfaced into the bar upstairs.

YE OLDE MITRE

The most secret pub in Cambridgeshire

1 Ely Court (entrance from Ely Place or between 9 & 10 Hatton Garden),
Farringdon, EC1N 6SJ
020 7405 4751
www.yeoldemitreholborn.co.uk
yeoldemitre@fullers.co.uk
Monday–Friday 11am–11pm
Tube station: Chancery Lane or Farringdon

"This is definitely London's most hidden pub," says John Wright, who served pints of real ale and toasted cheese sandwiches at Ye Olde Mitre for 27 years. Technically, this pub isn't in London at all. Originally built in 1546 for the servants of Ely Palace, London seat of the Bishop of Ely, it's still officially part of Cambridgeshire. Back in those days, England's bishops all had a residence in London because they sat in Parliament. Ely Palace was one of the grandest, with fountains, vineyards and strawberry fields stretching as far as the Thames.

Today's incarnation of Ye Olde Mitre dates from 1772, soon after Ely Palace was demolished. The wonky little pub is hidden down an alley linking Ely Place, a gated Georgian cul-de-sac, and Hatton Garden, an enclave of Jewish diamond dealers. The latter is named after Christopher Hatton, a mover and shaker in the court of Elizabeth I. In 1576, Hatton sweet-talked the Queen into leasing him a large part of Ely Palace for a yearly rent of one red rose, ten loads of hay and £10. Hatton later became Lord Chancellor, but didn't manage his own finances very well: he died owing the Crown £40,000.

In the pub's firelit front parlour is the preserved trunk of a cherry tree, which marked the boundary between Hatton's and the Bishop's property. Allegedly, Elizabeth I performed the maypole dance around this tree. Wooden settles and Tudor portraits line the mahogany-panelled back room, which leads to Ye Closet, a snug that merits the name. Barrels are dotted around the cloistered courtyard, an oasis on summer nights. The menu is as traditional as the interior: sandwiches, sausages, gherkins, and a fine selection of ales.

Sadly, beadles no longer call the hours or light the street lamps, but licensing hours are still fixed to the closing of the gates on Ely Place, so Ye Olde Mitre is shut at weekends. Until 1978, London's police could only enter Ely Place by invitation. "Criminals would run down the alley because the coppers couldn't follow them," Wright recalls. "They'd have to lock the gates and wait for reinforcements from Cambridge."

NEARBY

Le Café du Marché ⑧

Charterhouse Mews, 22 Charterhouse Square, Farringdon, EC1M 6DX
020 7608 1609
www.cafedumarche.co.uk

Hidden down a cobbled mews off Charterhouse Square, this très French restaurant has a loyal following. The set menu is hit-and-miss, but the authentically Gallic ambience is seductive. Le Grenier upstairs is perfect for clandestine trysts (and does excellent frites), occasionally accompanied by a jazz trio.

Pleasingly peculiar pubs

London is full of ancient and peculiar places to ponder your pint or neck your gin. If you've tried the pickled perfection of the Dog & Bell (page 184), the creative clutter of the Oxymoron (page 154), the hedonistic chaos of Ariadne's Nektar (page 102), the submersive sports collage of Woodies (page 212), the hidden wonkiness of Ye Olde Mitre (page 72), the faded glory of the Viaduct Tavern (page 70) and you've still got the legs for more – here are a few further stops to add into your beer crawl.

CITTIE OF YORKE
22 High Holborn WC1V 6BN – 020 7242 7670
At the back of this pub is a grand hall lined with ornately carved wooden booths, said to date from the 1600s. There used to be curtains over the entrance so that solicitors and barristers could have private conversations. Drinks were passed through little serving hatches now covered by copper plaques. Below is a huge long tunnel cellar where you can dine, drink and shelter from court orders.

SEVEN STARS
53 Carey Street, Temple, WC2A 2JB
020 7242 8521 – www.thesevenstars1602.co.uk
Any pub with a landlady named Roxy Beaujolais deserves patronage. Inspired by its location behind the Royal Courts of Justice, this snug watering hole is decorated with legal curiosities. Even the resident cat is usually dressed in a judge's ruff. The window displays ("cabinets of jurisprudence and largesse") contain arrangements of bewigged skulls and stuffed mice. At the back are possibly the most dangerous stairs in London. One of several contenders for the oldest pub in London, the Seven Stars miraculously survived the Great Fire of 1666, which broke out nearby.

SHERLOCK HOLMES
10-11 Northumberland Street, Westminster, WC2N 5DB
020 7930 2644 – www.sherlockholmespub.com
The mummified head of the Hound of the Baskervilles leers at the tourists sipping pints of Sherlock Holmes ale in the bar. But the real surprise is upstairs, where a faithful reproduction of Sherlock Holmes' study has been installed. Created for the 1951 Festival of Britain, this shrine to the fictional detective has been here ever since. You can peer at Holmes' violin, deerstalker and vials of borax through a glass wall in the restaurant. There's even a wax dummy of the detective with a bullet wound in his forehead. Of course, the real Holmes survived "to devote his life to examining those interesting little problems which the complex life of London so plentifully presents."

COCKPIT
7 St Andrews Hill, Blackfriars, EC4V 5BY – 020 7248 7315
"Any person with soiled clothing or dirty boots will not be served," says the off-putting sign outside this tiny corner pub, tucked away below St Paul's

Cathedral. This is a bit rich, since the pub smells of wee; but it's worth poking around, if only for its history. Built on the site of the gatehouse William Shakespeare bought in 1612, the pub used to be a cock-fighting arena (fights were held in the round saloon). Overhead is the gallery where bloodthirsty crowds gathered to watch the "sport" until it was banned in 1849. Traces of a Roman pizza parlour have also been unearthed on the site.

WILLIAMSON'S TAVERN

1 Groveland Court, off Bow Lane, EC4M 9EH
020 7248 5750 — www.nicholsonspubs.co.uk

The official residence of the Lord Mayor of London until Mansion House was built in 1753, Williamson's held the first excise licence in the City of London. Allegedly, an ancient marker denoting the dead centre of the City lies somewhere on the premises, but none of the staff know where it is. Browse the bound collection of the Illustrated London News and read all about the new "asylum for idiots" in Highgate or "the increase of pauperism" in 1849.

MORPETH ARMS

58 Millbank, Pimlico, SW1P 4RW
020 7834 6442 — www.morpetharms.com

Tate Britain was built on the site of Millbank prison, the first national penitentiary founded in 1816. Sadly, Jeremy Bentham's revolutionary "panopticon" design did not live up to his ideals of social reform. Henry James called Millbank "a worse act of violence than any it was erected to punish." Convicts bound for deportation to Australia were shuffled through a series of underground tunnels connecting the jail to the riverbank. A section of tunnel survives in the cellars of the Morpeth Arms, a pub built to serve the prison warders and allegedly haunted by the ghost of a former inmate.

BLIND BEGGAR

337 Whitechapel Rd, Whitechapel, E1 1BU
020 7247 6195 — www.theblindbeggar.com

William Booth, founder of the Salvation Army, preached his first sermon outside the Beggar. But the pub is notorious for a more degenerate incident: in 1966, East End gangster Ronnie Kray walked into the bar and shot George Cornell dead. The record playing on the jukebox was *The Sun Ain't Gonna Shine Anymore* by the Walker Brothers.

FREEMASONS ARMS

32 Downshire Hill, Hampstead, NW3 1NT
020 7433 6811 — www.freemasonsarms.co.uk

The beer garden beside Hampstead Heath is always heaving in summer, but the cellar of this rather corporate boozer is home to London's last surviving skittles club. The object of this traditional pub game is to knock down nine pins by lobbing (rather than rolling) a "cheese" (actually a thudding great ball of lignum vitae). Matches are held on Tuesday evenings. There has been a skittles alley at The Freemasons Arms since the 19th century.

HESTER'S HIDEOUT

The hoochiest of the coochiest

Basement of 2 Exmouth Market, Clerkenwell, EC1R 4PX
020 7837 7139
hestershideout.com
Monday–Thursday 5pm–12am, Friday–Saturday 5pm–2.30am
Burlesque cabaret Friday and Saturday from 8pm; booking essential
Tube station: Farringdon, Angel or King's Cross

Hester's Hideout is in a basement on the corner of Exmouth Market and Farringdon Road. The only clue that you've got the right building is a curlicued "H" etched into the glass of a no entry door. Eventually you figure it out: the entrance is through Paesan, the large bright Italian trattoria where families and friends are eating tasteful platters of antipasti and big bowls of traditional pasta.

Photos by Jan Pearson

But descend the internal stairs and you find yourself in an entirely different atmosphere. Restraint is not the byword here. Bawdy might be. The cocktails are full strength, and at the weekends the entertainment is in your face. Literally. The great thing about Hester's is how close up it all is. There's no stage separating the performers from the audience, the singing and dancing is right up in your personal space.

On Sneak Easy Fridays, the Vaudevillian Mister Meredith is at the piano, belting out saucy ballads with a smattering of enthusiastic tap dancing, his steel-tipped brogues perilously close to your face. Then out swings Hannah Lou, a barefoot Carmen Miranda (sans fruit bowl) who shimmies into the snugs and lures out guests with her hypnotising hips.

Though the audience, it must be said, don't need much persuasion. They are thoroughly game. Maybe it's the cocktails. Or maybe it's the way Marlene Cheaptrick balances a martini on her head while performing a handstand, shooting poppers from her bra and singing an uncensored version of "Falling in Love Again".

A Chinese whisper game starts off with "I love your cock;" heaven knows where it can go from there. One gentleman seems quite content to submit to wearing Marlene's fur stole as a wig while she does a headstand on his crotch, her legs wide open below his chin. Deux Ailes perform erotic lesbian gymnastics; at this distance, you can see the veins straining around one Elle's extraordinarily strong arms. By the end of the night, everyone is up dancing. And it's all got a bit non sequitur. One gent gives us his top tips on how to dry the testicles with a special walk. Another gets into an in-depth marriage therapy session with a stranger.

I am reminded of Dorothy Parker's warnings about the perils of more than two cocktails. But you can rest assured that if you do end up under your host, it will probably be as part of a burlesque stage trick. And that's only Fridays. Apparently Saturdays are the really wild nights.

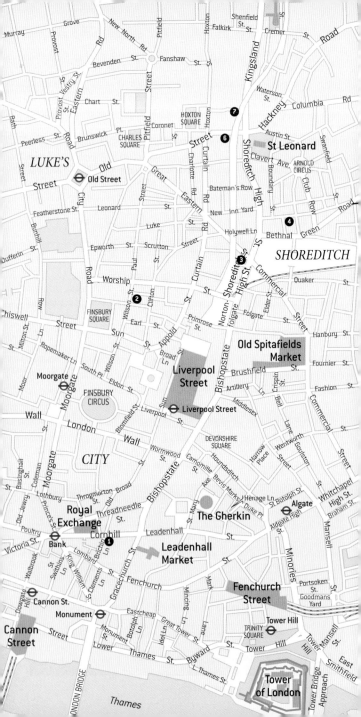

Tower Bridge to Shoreditch

SIMPSON'S TAVERN

Guess the stewed cheese

Ball Court, 38½ Cornhill, City of London, EC3V 9DR
020 7626 9985
www.simpsonstavern.co.uk
manager@simpsonstavern.co.uk
Monday—Friday 12pm—3pm, breakfast Tuesday—Friday 8am —11am
Bar: 11.30am—3.30pm
Tube station: Bank

Chicken and ham pie on Monday, cottage pie on Tuesday, roast beef with Yorkshire pudding ... If this sounds like your school dinner rota, don't be alarmed. The daily specials at Simpson's Tavern, which haven't changed for 260 years, are tastier than anything you were force-fed at school. If you want to ring the changes, there's plenty more "good honest fare": chump chops, bubble and squeak, stilton and tawny port for dessert. The house speciality, "Stewed Cheese", is a must: a hot pot of melted, mustardy cheese is served on top of a slice of toast. Just add Worcester sauce and a dash of red pepper.

The address, 38½ Cornhill, isn't the only thing out of the ordinary about this 18th-century chophouse hidden down a narrow passageway. Thomas Simpson opened his Fish Ordinary Restaurant in Billingsgate market in 1723. He established a tradition, sadly now defunct, of "guessing the cheese". A whole cheese was wheeled in; whoever guessed the correct weight was treated to champagne and cigars. Simpson moved to this site in 1757. The original wooden booths, with brass rails to hang your bowler hat, can be wobbly when the portly punters have had too many pints. You have to share with strangers, which encourages plenty of boozy banter.

"What's an Edwardian pork chop?"

"It's very old – like the waitresses."

"Have you worked here long?"

"Not really – only 40 years," quips Maureen, still with a twinkle in her eye at 80.

Simpson's was the first establishment in London to employ female waitresses. Kiri and Tina, a matronly duo in twinsets and pearls, cluck over their "boys" (most of whom are over 60) like mother hens. Jean has been holding court in the basement bar for over 30 years. Yet female patrons were only admitted to the restaurant in 1916. The City traders still seem ruffled whenever I slide into a booth.

Once upon a time, two shillings would buy "the original fish dinner at 1 o'clock" – soup, four fish courses, two meat courses, bread, cheese and salad. Prices have gone up, but it's still remarkably reasonable. I guess the owners make all their money on booze: customers put away 50 boxes of wine a week, and it's only open for lunch, Monday to Friday. Friday lunchtime is liveliest, but do book ahead. Or you could write off the day even earlier with a "Full English" breakfast and a killer Bloody Mary.

BLACK ROCK,
SACK & THE DEVIL'S DARLING

Three's company

Napoleon Hotel, 9 Christopher Street, Hackney EC2A 2BS
020 3246 0045; www.napoleon-hotel.com
Black Rock: 020 7247 4580; hello@blackrock.bar
Sack: 0203 246 0045; Sack.mail@sack.bar
The Devil's Darling: 020 3633 1006; hello@napoleon-hotel.com
Monday—Saturday 5pm—late
Tube station: Moorgate or Liverpool Street

Photo by Addie Chinn

The back streets around the City are strangely dead at weekends, when the high financiers head to their low country pads for rest and relaxation. But on the corner of Christopher Street there's a single luxury hotel suite above a trio of bars to lure rogue traders to stay in the City for a Saturday threesome.

Floating on the top layer is The Devil's Darling cocktail bar – the name references a satirical sketch of the Devil cradling the infant Napoleon. A barman mixes your classic cocktail – there are only ever three on the menu – from a long green marble bar. Behind him hangs a huge painting of Napoleon's coronation. Sip your mix at a starch-linened table and peer into your reflection in the little green crystal-cut lampshade.

Or venture downstairs to the surprising middle layer: an Andalusian bodega called Sack (a fortified white wine imported from Spain: a historical corruption of Sec). Here you can drink all types of sherry, cocktails made of sherry, and even sherry slushies – one of which was surprisingly good, so much so that I can't remember which one. To aid your selective memory there's a great pictogram on the wall, which places the brands of sherry on the spectrums of dry, nut, fruit and sweet. Seventies dance music on the decks, a few simple tapas to snack on – jamón, boquerones, smoked almonds. Why go any further?

But you should, because the most dramatic layer is saved for last. Lurking in the dark subterranean bowels is the Black Rock whisky bar. Down the middle of the basement is a long table made of the spliced trunk of a 185-year-old oak tree, with two parallel channels running the full length. One channel, lined with American wood, contains the house blend of whisky; in the other, lined with French limousine, the house cocktail is mellowing. Taps at the end. Glass on top. Eighteen strangers can sit around this and get to know each other, along with the vast selection of whiskies … though you don't have to blend, there are also smaller tables at the side.

Order from your seat or wander up and choose your dram from three double cabinets, the bottles arranged according to character: smoky or fruity, balanced or fragrant, sweet or spicy. And if you need something to soak it all up, there's a selection of Celtic snacks – haggis balls, oysters, soda bread, cured salmon. Or perhaps just ask the staff to load you into the dumb waiter and send you up to the penthouse suite.

LOUNGE BOHEMIA

Underground paean to mid-century modern

1e Great Eastern Street, Shoreditch, EC2A 3EJ
07720 707000
www.loungebohemia.com
Monday–Saturday 6pm–12am, Sunday 6pm–11pm
Tube station: Old Street

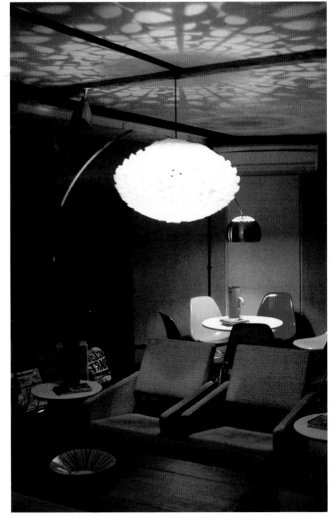

It takes brass to call a kebab shop the Savoy and it takes a bold bartender to create a cocktail bar that's by appointment only. Paul Tvaroh's Lounge Bohemia is hidden in a basement below the Corner Savoy takeaway, but you won't get in without calling ahead. The "no standing, no suits" policy means that it's never crowded and the clientele is infallibly cool.

The bearded, brooding Tvaroh, who really is from Bohemia in the Czech Republic, spent months searching for a venue. "I noticed the shutters one day and wondered what was on the other side … It was an abandoned Chinese restaurant with some very scary-looking ingredients that had been left behind. It took a lot of TLC to get it to where it is now."

A barely lit corridor plastered with Czech newspapers leads to a secret lair dedicated to molecular mixology and mid-century modern design. The bar is constructed from furniture that belonged to Tvaroh's grandmother. Menus are hidden in vintage hardbacks, prohibition style. While you investigate the intriguing cocktail list, the waitress brings water and smoked paprika popcorn. The jazz soundtrack is never too loud – this is a place for serious conversation as well as seriously experimental drinkers.

There's absinthe in various guises and a long collection of rare spirits. But the real draw is Tvaroh's extraordinary selection of dramatic cocktails, based on in-house syrups and infusions. There's Stolichnaya vodka infused with poppy seed or porcini, Czech rum infused with bacon, and Cuban rum infused with a Romeo & Juliet cigar. Syrups are flavoured with Jack Daniel's oak barrel chippings, cinnamon bark and parma violet.

Molecular cocktails are as much about overturning expectation as theatrical presentation. Holy Smoke (leather infused cognac, frankincense and myrrh smoke, served in a gold glass holder) was inspired by the three kings and their gifts. The "nature" tasting menu includes an elaborate candyfloss sculpture made from crystallised becherovka, a Czech digestive liqueur with spicy undertones of cloves and cinnamon. "Everyone expects the candyfloss to be very sweet, when it fact it's quite bitter with a kick to

it," says Tvaroh. The candy floss creations don't end there, Tvaroh has developed numerous flavours for different cocktails. "I probably have the only bar in London where the candy floss machine takes pride of place."

Pssssst... please tell everyone
Speakeasy bars

Since the first edition of this book, London has gone Speakeasy crazy. The post-modern Prohibition craze started in New York's East Village at the beginning of the new century with hard-to-find retro-style bars like 'Milk & Honey' and 'Please Don't Tell', accessed via an old phone booth in a hot dog joint. It caught on in London when **Milk & Honey** members' club opened up in Poland Street in 2002. The next year, **Trailer Happiness** opened an underground Trader Vic's style tiki bar on Portobello Road. Soon the Breakfast Club created their first secret bar, **The Mayor of Scaredy Cat Town**, accessed via a fridge in their Spitalfields branch.

Now those once secret places are world famous and there's hardly a basement, back room or bog that hasn't been redecorated with vintage styling, an obscure entrance way and an experimental mixologist crafting a themed and highly instagrammable cocktail list. Some copy the American romance with Prohibition, but since the Brits were never so rash as to try and ban alcohol, the tendency is towards wartime rationing or general retro fun and glamour. The cynic in me says these are just a way of keeping prices high (cocktails are usually around the £12 mark) and the riff raff out. And maybe strangers on Tinder dates need more immediate things to talk about. But eradicating the need for visibility allows smaller independent bars to set up in affordable locations. And the places are so creative, the atmosphere so fun and the drinks so goddamn delicious that I'm nearly always won over.

Kath Morell of surrealist toyland **Ninety Eight Bar & Lounge** on Curtain Road reckons the fashion has been fuelled by people wanting to escape their characterless offices and recapture some of their childhood sense of fun. If you're going to splash some cash on a special night out, you might as well have your drink expertly mixed and served in extraordinary surrounds. There are so many speakeasies in London that we couldn't possibly list them all, but here are a few clandestine cocktail curios for you to track down – remember that with most you need to book in advance on their website or the guy on the door might well deny all knowledge of their existence.

CENTRE
- Off Carnaby Street, you can get a taste of British Blitz Spirit in **Cahoots** (page 20) or there's a sixties Manhattan elegance in **Disrepute**.
- **Purl** spin multisensory molecular cocktails in Marleylebone.
- Look under the old "Optician" sign on Poland Street to find gangster chic at the **Blind Pig**.
- Shock onlookers by walking into triple-X-rated **La Bodega Negra** (page 30).
- At the end of the Strand, you'll find performances in the toilets at the **Cellardoor** (page 66).

NORTH

- A little north of the centre on Exmouth Market, you can find saucy vaudevillian entertainment in **Hester's Hideout** (page 76).
- In Stoke Newington, **Original Sin** hides its pool table beneath a burger bar, and you can find flapper glamour at **Ruby's Bar**.
- The lantern outside tells you you've found the bar with no name – aka **69 Colebrooke Row**, which mixes 1950s Italian Café style with film noir.
- The **Ladies & Gentlemen** toilets on the crossroads above Kentish Town tube are actually a tiny cellar bar.

SOUTH

- In Brixton, the **Courtesan** has a late-night weekend cocktail bar, hidden below its dim sum tea rooms, mixing spirits made by female distillers.
- In Balham, you can'll find the **Owl**, a tiny cellar bar down the spiral staircase inside Foxlow's.
- There's a sliding wall in Battersea's Breakfast Club launderette leading into the **King Of Ladies Man**, a 1970s style bachelor pad. They also have a place in London Bridge where, if you tell the waitress "I'm here to get lucky," you'll be escorted through to **Call Me Mr Lucky**.

EAST

- **Callooh Callay** has a backroom bar filled with trompe l'oeil mirrors and an even more secret upstairs **Jubjub** members' bar for "friends and family."
- Slum it Victorian style in the **Worship Street Whistling Shop** grand gin palace.
- In the space below Smithfield Market where the Cock Tavern once hid, **Oriole** has replicated the jazz and cocktails formula originated by its sister venue, the **Nightjar**.
- Head through a corner kebab shop into **Lounge Bohemia** (page 84) for theatrical molecular cocktails.
- **TT Liquor** – have a hidden bar in the old prison cells below their recherché drink shop. Upstairs you can learn to be a bartender in their cocktail school.
- Pull up on your motorbike outside '50s greasy-spoon **Jim's Café** in Clapton and discover a high-end cocktail bar with great food.

WEST

- **Evans & Peel** have two Prohibition-themed places: a **Detective Agency** in Earls Court where you present your case to a Sam Spade before going through to their speakeasy. And a **Pharmacy** in Chiswick where you must explain your medical condition to a nurse before they let you in.
- Confess your soon-to-be-committed sins in the basement of a Portobello pintxo bar at **Pix Confessional**.
- In Chelsea, you can play dressing up at **Barts** (page 132) or at being cowboys in the **Moonshine Saloon**.
- And in Fulham, the flatmates behind the **Little Blue Door** will throw you a house party, where ladies can go two by two to the loos.

WALLUC

An homage to fromage

40 Redchurch Street, E2 7DP
07864 219140 (text only)
Most evenings from 7pm but text to check
Tube station: Shoreditch High Street or Liverpool Street

A rriving at Walluc is like walking into an Aki Kaurasmäki film set: a small front room filled with scruffy chairs, guitars, fishing nets, two or three motorbikes, and staffed by a couple of rockabillies in turn-up jeans. In the background, a washing line is pegged with clothes. In fact, the film reference is very specific: owner Luca's inspiration is from the classic *Trilogie Marseillaise,* three acclaimed films (*Marius, Fanny* and *César*) set around the port city of Marseille and made in the 1930s by Marcel Pagnol, considered France's first cinematic genius. The restaurant defies Shoreditch's hipster norms. There is no website or even an email. You need to text to book a table (not phone) as Luca might be on his motorbike.

The hours are unreliable; the heating, lighting or coffee machine may be on the blink. Some sheets of kitchen paper serve as napkins. The menu is short. It's basically melted cheese – fondue or raclette; charcuterie to start, a salad to accompany. There are four or five wines on the list, all the same price. Service is laid-back: you might get chatting to Luca for a while before he heads down the steep stairs to melt more cheese. If you ask for something that's not on the menu, he'll probably nip out and buy it for you from a nearby shop.

My barrister friend and I have chosen the fondue, and she tolerates my cheese puns while we await the hotting pot. Listen Caerphilly. Best cheese for blindfolding a horse? Mascarpone. Who am I to dis a brie?, etc. etc. Her diet is vegetarian and gluten free, but that's no problem – I'd texted that request ahead and Luca had located vegetarian cheese and some delicious crusty gluten-free bread, along with simple new potatoes, boiled to the right soft-but-firmness. The *pot au fromage* is placed over a grid of tea candles and we get a bucket of spikey bread-wrangling tools. It's perfect gooey yumminess, provoking an unspoken cheese race.

My legal friend cunningly distracts me with short but open questions, and dives in for a solo cheese spree while I attempt to answer. But then blinded by candlelight, she makes the rookie error of losing her bread chunk. I swiftly make up for lost cheese time while she frantically rotates through implements to fish out the escapee cube. By the time we've reached the golden crust at the bottom of the Le Creuset, it's a satisfying dead heat (a feta compli if you will).

LADY DINAH'S CAT EMPORIUM

Through the Looking Glass

152–154 Bethnal Green Road, E2 6DG
www.ladydinahs.com
bookings@ladydinahs.co.uk
Monday –Sunday 10/11am–6pm; closed Wednesday
Tube station: Shoreditch High Street or Liverpool Street

Photos by Mona Sosa

There's a cat sat on the mat in the window of 154 Bethnal Green Road. She stares through the glass at the strange urban zoo outside: hipsters, stall holders, baristas, publicans, nail technicians, stock brokers – all jostling with each other to be leader of the pack in the ever-changing East End marketplace.

On the other side of the looking glass is a place where cats are the undisputed overlords. You can come and hang out with them if you like, in their Alice in Wonderland themed play park, with its hidden underground rabbit hole and ceiling-height catwalks. Book in for tea and cakes and mere mortals get to wander freely among all fourteen of them – pet them, play with them, parlay with them, take endless pictures with them. Meet Lizzie, who likes to run on the cat wheel and won't share. Carbonelle, who dangles her paw as she gazes disdainfully down from an overhead shelf. And Wookie, who's partial to the smell of sweaty armpits. They've got the humans like putty in their claws.

Cat cafés are big in Japan. That's where founder Lauren Pears first encountered one and thought the idea might work well in London. Like many in the city, she didn't have a big enough apartment to keep a pet and missed the cats she'd grown up with at home in Australia. A café where you can drop in for an hour or two's feline fix would be … purrfect. Couple that with the whole (slightly inexplicable) internet cat craze and you've got yourself a fully crowdfunded first cat café in the UK, booked from dawn till dusk. Clever girl …

All the cats at Lady Dinah's are rescue cats, none of them thoroughbreds. There's a dedicated cat carer on the staff to ensure the animals are treated well, and cat checks are performed every four hours. Visitors develop

strong relationships with them, following them on Instagram or joining the café's foster network. One devoted lady flies in twice a year from Vienna.

So long as you don't pester them when they're sleeping or washing, the cats enjoy the stimulation of human company.

Wookie likes them so much that he hides when the closing-time cat check is done, so that the staff have to stay behind trying to coax him out with treats. But overnight, when all the humans are gone, that's when the cat party really gets wild.

ZIFERBLAT

About time

388 Old Street, Shoreditch, EC1V 9LT
07984 693 440
london.ziferblat.net
ziferblat.london@gmail.com
Monday–Friday 10am–11pm, Saturday and Sunday 12pm–11pm
7p/minute for 1ˢᵗ hour; 4p/minute thereafter; daily cap at 4ᵗʰ hour: £11.40
Tube station: Hoxton, Old Street or Shoreditch High Street

Above a pub on the corner of Old Street is a café where the drinks are free. At Ziferblat, instead of paying for what you consume, you pay for the time you spend there. Take a clock as you enter and then help yourself to the cappuccino machine, slices of cake, jars of muesli and bowls of fresh fruit. It's a lovely homely space, decorated with drawings of clocks. Big windows fill the room with light and frame the Hoxton sunset. Dotted around the place are friendly handwritten signs on brown cardboard, telling you what events are coming up, how to use the coffee machine. One explains that if your biscuit seems damp, not to worry, it'll just be one that's been specially pre-licked.

You'd think the ticking clock might add to the stress but the vibe is relaxed studious. A co-working space with wifi, chargers and a printer

available for free. Perfect for when you're getting cabin fever at home. Or perhaps the heating is on the blink. Or they're drilling outside. Or you want to kill your flatmate/children/the men with drills … It's also a social space – there are exhibitions, poetry evenings, music jams. Saturday games night can get pretty rowdy. If you want to escape, have a private conversation or just feel like a nap, there's a secret room off to the side, decked out with beanbags (plus the vacuum cleaner – it's really a storage room).

If this all seems unusually egalitarian, then that's because it was started in Russia by a group of friends with a secret poetry project: to leave poems written on little cards all over Moscow. But when they gathered in cafés to make the cards, staff kept interrupting with heavy hints to buy more coffees and questions about what they were up to with their laminating machines and paper trimmers.

The group needed somewhere to work uninterrupted by the pressure to consume. And so they started the first Ziferblat, a sharing space for creative work. Initially the rent was covered by voluntary donations, but it got so popular that they had to expand. And formalise the financing. But the collective, community spirit remains. If you're low on funds, you can earn more time by taking out the trash, manning the reception, downloading their app. And the guest book is filled with highly artistic entries, proving what you can achieve if you've got time on your hands.

THE BRIDGE

An endless American Dream

15 Kingsland Road, Shoreditch, E2 8AA
020 3489 2216
facebook.com/thebridge15
hasan1991@hotmail.co.uk
Thursday, Friday and Sunday 5pm—1.30am, Saturday 5pm—2.30am
Tube station: Hoxton

I t's very easy to miss The Bridge … on account of it being under a bridge. If you pass by during office hours, it is shrouded in gloom, shuttered-up and hiding from the day like a work-shy, narcoleptic vampire. But as dark approaches, a cluster of neon signs light up and start to shine from the little window, announcing the availability of liquor. And one by one, passers-by are lured inside, like moths to an electric flame …

Once the door closes behind you, and you become accustomed to the dimness, you realise that the narrow downstairs bar is stashed full of vintage memorabilia. Every inch of the wall hypnotises you with '70s telephones, photos of boxers, adverts for old-fashioned drinks, clocks, lamps. Intrigued, you move further into the bar, maybe order a drink from the handsome, friendly young barman. He hands you a beer, which has been iced in a 1940s Coca-Cola chest freezer. Or he makes you an espresso – better still, an espresso martini – using a shiny 1960s Elektra coffee machine. He rings up your bill on a 19th-century cash register from Dayton, Ohio. You sip your drink, your eyes flicking from one object to the next. Another neon sign by the stairs flashes "Girls Girls Girls" and lures you still further into the depths. A hidden door to the side swings open to reveal yet another room, filled with vintage Americana: motel and gas station signs, tables and tin logos, all bathed in a dark red light which lulls you into an old American Dream. Sit down, rest your feet, have some food, some sweet pie? It's so very relaxed in here, there's really no need to get up …

Maybe you muster enough energy to re-emerge. But wait, surely you cannot resist a quick look upstairs? As you reach the top of the stairs, you encounter perhaps the most rococo room in existence. Ornate, velvet-covered chaises longues and Louis XIV armchairs are lit by glowing Tiffany lamps, reflected eternally in dark, gilt-edged mirrors. The urge to sit down is irresistible. As you sink into the heavy comfort and the soft music, the idea of leaving becomes a dim and distant memory.

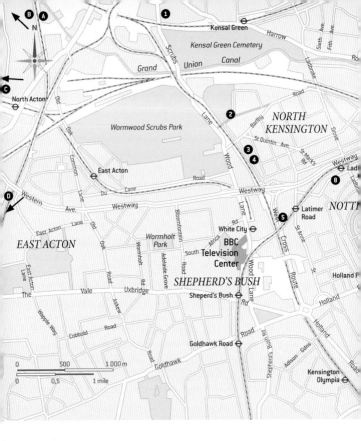

Marylebone to Shepherd's Bush

CENTRO GALEGO DE LONDRES ①

Top-class tapas at knockdown prices

869 Harrow Road, Willesden, NW10 5NG
020 8964 4873
www.restaurantecentrogalego.london
Tuesday–Friday 12pm–10.30pm, Saturday 1pm–11pm, Sunday 1pm–9pm
Tube/Rail station: Willesden Junction

Stretching from Edgware Road to Willesden, Harrow Road is one of those dreary expanses of no man's land that Londoners drive through in a hurry. But there are a few nuggets of culinary brilliance lodged between the pound shops and fried chicken joints. On a particularly desolate strip, where Harrow Road tails off into Harlesden, this cosy social club is where Galician expats gather to gossip over giant portions of authentic Spanish food.

It doesn't look like much from the outside. But pull up a stool at the tapas bar and there's an unmistakable air of Mediterranean bonhomie, from the generous glug of Rias Baixas to the bulging basket of bread and butter. Through the kitchen hatch, you can watch the chefs slicing fluffy mounds of boiled potatoes to turn into a moist, melting tortilla – a treat that's often thrown in free with your first glass of wine.

At the handful of tables, stocky Spaniards tuck into enormous plates of paella and steaks the size of skis. I prefer to sample as many dishes as possible from the selection of fantastic and fantastically cheap tapas. Despite several visits with equally voracious friends, I haven't managed to try everything. However, I can wholeheartedly recommend the *pulpo con cachelos* (boiled octopus and potatoes dusted with rock salt and smoked paprika), *pimientos de padron* (flash-fried baby peppers that will occasionally blow your head off), and *chorizo al vino* (punchy garlic sausage cooked in Rioja). Seafood is a Galician speciality and my prawn-loving pals go crazy for the *gambas al ajillo* (garlicky tails of king prawn).

Downstairs are two larger dining rooms that appear to be trapped in Spanish suburbia circa 1980 (napkin fans, random folk art, trophies from the resident football club, Deportivo Galicia, founded in 1968 like the Centro Galego itself). On Friday and Saturday nights, diners are entertained with (deafening) live music. One evening in August, I stumbled upon a traditional festival, with revellers in horned helmets playing the bagpipes. Apparently, this raucous ritual commemorates Galicia's Celtic roots.

The best time to visit is during a football match featuring any Spanish team. Crowded into every corner are extended families in football strips, men chewing over tactics between mouthfuls of monkfish stew, anxious fans knocking back Estrella beers. The whole place erupts whenever the Spaniards score and if the right team wins you'll be hugging and dancing with strangers. I can't wait for the next World Cup.

FITOU'S

Park Thai

1–3 Dalgarno Gardens, North Kensington, W10 5LL
020 8968 0558
www.fitourestaurant.co.uk
fitousthairestaurant@gmail.com
Tuesday–Sunday 12pm–3pm, 6pm–10.30pm
Tube station: White City or Latimer Road
Buses: 7, 70, 220

Fitou's was the first restaurant I went to on the night I moved from Scotland to London. Too shattered to cook, my friend and I could just about make it round the corner to this unassuming little neighbourhood restaurant. Hidden in back streets not far from the old BBC TV Centre, it's on the edge of Little Wormwood Scrubs park, where travellers once pastured their ponies, inspiring Galton and Simpson's sitcom, *Steptoe and Son*.

Number 1 Thai Café, as it was called at the time, was cheap and it was BYOB. Perfect. Order – nip out for a couple of bottles of lager from the corner shop next door – sorted. We weren't after anything special, just something hot and fast enough that we could eat before collapsing on the plate. But when the starters arrived, we began to perk up. You could tell by the delicate flavour and the crunch of water chestnuts that the steamed chicken dumplings were handmade. Little sweetcorn fritters were also surprisingly good – crispy, light and chewy, with a tasty homemade chilli fish sauce. This was not what we had been expecting. The mains were even better – a whole pomfret fish in thick hot red *Gaeng Panang* curry sauce was exceptional, accompanied by sticky rice, a rarity on menus at the time. My friend's *Pad Thai* was perfect. The staff were friendly, the chef was a lovely Thai lady called Tou, and the place seemed to be full of a great mix of people: my new neighbours. This was going to be a good move.

Over a decade later, both restaurant and park have had makeovers, but the dishes are still as good, the prices are great, and the regulars are still me and the neighbours. Tou is still in the kitchen and her friendly nephew Killan is front of house. He'll even pass your plates out the French windows if you want to eat at the picnic tables on the edge of the park.

NEARBY
The Fusion by Kai ③
308 Latimer Road, North Kensington, W10 6QW
020 3784 3105
www.thefusionbykailatimer.co.uk
Terrible name and fairly standard Thai dishes, but a beautiful tiny restaurant hiding under a canopy of ivy – you feel like you're hiding in someone's secret garden.

ARIADNE'S NEKTAR

Master and moussaka

274 Latimer Road, North Kensington, W10 6QU
020 8968 8212
www.facebook.com/ariadnesnectar
Daily 10pm–12am; call ahead to check
Tube station: White City or Latimer Road

The first clue that this isn't your typical boozer are the two motorbikes parked inside. Then there's the photograph of the naked landlord astride one of them hanging by the toilets. Ariadne's Nektar is the kind of place where someone might stroll up to the bar in a gorilla suit (which happened to me one night). It's a seemingly low-key bar where you strike up conversations with strangers, accidentally get slaughtered on a Monday night, and end up necking your neighbour (which happened to a friend of mine).

The maverick behind this work of genius is Dimitri, the most irascible landlord in London. A former lawyer who enjoys modelling his collection of wigs and hats, Dimitri likes nothing better than a fierce debate (as long as he wins the argument). Just don't get him started on Greek etymology or the politics of civil disobedience. If he's in a good mood, Dimitri will break out his stash of *tsipouro* (Cretan grappa) and home-cured olives. If you inadvertently rile him, he will treat you to "a bollocking free of charge." Anyone who has spent time in Greece will appreciate that this particular form of abuse is usually reserved for favoured patrons.

Named after Dimitri's beautiful daughter, Ariadne's Nektar is a local in the real sense of the word. With its ragged collection of antiques and cosy lighting, it's like straying into someone's living room. The usual suspects propping up the bar are bohemian local residents, pretty things from the textile design studio next door, and musicians stumbling in after a session at The Grove recording studios across the road. Occasionally, bands stage live shows or impromptu jam sessions in the pub. Otherwise, patrons are well served by Dimitri's sweeping music collection, which ranges from Gorillaz to Dizzy Gillespie.

The legendary Thursday night pub quiz is sadly now a rare occurrence, but now they serve Greek food, smoothies and coffees all day long. In summer you can quaff margaritas and mojitos, made with generous Mediterranean-style measures, at the handful of tables outside. After too many cocktails, fortify yourself with Dimitri's delicious spanakopitta and moussaka. Dimitri keeps threatening to sell up and retire to a Greek island, so go and experience his unconventional hospitality while you can. But be warned: the opening hours are as unpredictable as the owner.

PRINCESSE D'ISENBOURG ET CIE ⑤

Withnail's finest foods

2 Bard Road, Holland Park, W10 6TP
020 8960 3600
caviar.co.uk
caviar@caviar.co.uk
Monday–Friday 10am–6.30pm, Saturday 10am–12.30pm
Tube station: Latimer Road, Shepherd's Bush or Holland Park

I first stumbled upon Princesse d'Isenbourg when I was researching the filming locations of *Withnail & I* for a Movie Trails phone app. This industrial cul-de-sac was where the degenerate duo Withnail and Marwood set off on their drive to Penrith. Knocking on a warehouse door to ask if the owners knew of the filming, I was greeted by a dapper gentleman called Gunther. And invited in to the most unexpected lock-up I had ever seen.

Princesse d'Isenbourg et Cie is steered by Persian-German team, Pari and Gunther, and they have turned this place into a fine food cathedral. Erté ladies hang on high banners over a grand hall. Classical music fills the air. Down the centre is a long table made out of a *pupitre* – an angle-slotted holder for turning champagne bottles. A golden stuffed sturgeon from Shilat, the Iranian ministry of fishing, top shelves draped with fishing nets and covered with fine food paraphernalia. And also French dolls house furniture … And also a copper diving helmet … There's a kind of fishy foodie French connection running through them all but sometimes the link gets a bit tenuous. "It's a very abnormal office," smiles Pari. "Much was collected on business trips, but people also keep giving us things. We tell them please stop but …" and she gestures to a side table displaying a rubber Pink Panther doll. Then she jumps to her feet and points out a table made of beautiful old blue Persian caviar tins. "If you grow up by the Caspian Sea, caviar is just a normal thing to eat. Like oysters were in Britain." Catching wild sturgeon was banned in 2006, so all the caviar they sell is sustainably farmed. There is a hyper-clean packing room in the back, with a chilled stainless-steel operating table and their special tins and labels. They are the only company with their own champagne and caviar label. They also sell saffron, foie gras, truffles and more. If you come to taste, you are expected to buy, and of course none of this costs pennies – note the prices on the website. For a very special celebration, you can make a caviar dinner reservation, but we're talking well over £100 per guest. Their clients are VIPs and they will not name any, though I suspect a former prime minister to be amongst them. Certainly Withnail would have felt very happy here.

NEARBY

Caviar Artisan (6)

272 Kensington Church St, Notting Hill, W8 4DP
020 7846 0024
caviarartisan.com

If you aren't quite sure if you're ready to invest, you can more casually drop in on this lovely little Iranian delicatessen and café which has a wall decorated with old caviar tins, serves delicious salads, cakes and teas (the saffron tea is amazing) and has a caviar-tasting cellar room below.

PORTOBELLO GARDEN CAFFÈ

Hidden Italy

Portobello Arcade, 269b Portobello Road, W11 1LR
020 7792 8419
www.facebook.com/Portobello-Garden-Caffe-654459517967701
italiancafe@portobellogardencafe.co.uk
Monday—Sunday 10am—10pm
Tube station: Ladbroke Grove or Notting Hill Gate

The first time I found Portobello Garden Caffè was when my car had broken down nearby. Killing time while I waited for the recovery

company, I wandered into one of the arcades on Portobello Road, browsing vintage clothes, and spotted a door hidden at the back. Inside was a wonderful glass-ceilinged slice of old-style Italia with prosciutto hams hanging from the ceiling and shelves piled high with fresh cheeses, cured meats and trays of homemade antipasti preserves: colourful peppers, soft artichoke hearts and glistening olives.

As I sipped a cappuccino, a little 5-year-old girl who was also killing time decided to draw me pictures of her favourite animals. She also pointed out her Mamma and her Nonna, who were serving in the caffè. Her Pappa was working behind the door. This, it turned out, was the Ferro family from Sorrento, the beautiful coastal town just south of Naples. Pappa – aka Franco – runs the Saporitalia restaurant, not exactly behind the door but just across the road, and Mamma – Mariella – had branched out and started this caffè in 2014. She was worried that people wouldn't find it: it was too hidden. But slowly, through word of mouth, customers started to step through the door and discover the beautiful décor and amazing freshly made saltimbocca sandwiches, which do just what their name tells you – jump in the mouth.

The kitchen itself is a sandwich, a narrow gap into which the staff disappear every now and then and emerge carrying steaming plates of *parmigiana di melanzane* or fragrant *paccheri quattro formaggi e tartufo*. "The only English thing on the menu is the tap water," says Mariella, "everything else is Italian." Perhaps the most interesting dish is *salsiccia con scamorza e friarielli* (sausage, smoked cheese and broccoli), something that only the Neapolitans cook: Italians from other regions stare at you blankly if you ask about it.

This is where I go on a cold grey afternoon when I feel the winter is lasting too long – it always manages to feel bright and summery inside. If you visit at Christmas time, there are pretty panettone boxes hanging everywhere. It looks like the arcade hiding the front is changing, it may not be vintage clothes that cloak the entranceway for long. And I suspect that Mariella's daughter may have grown out of drawing animals. But the Garden Caffè is still one of the most special places on Portobello Road.

NEARBY

Museum of Brands Garden Café   ⑧

111–117 Lancaster Road, Portobello, W11 1QT
0207 2439 611
www.museumofbrands.com

Hiding in the back of the excellent Museum of Brands, Packaging and Advertising is a little café which not only lets you see some of the museum's fun displays, but also has a wonderful tropical garden, beautifully maintained for over 30 years by gardener Gary Eisenhauer.

BOOKS FOR COOKS

Try before you buy

4 Blenheim Crescent, Notting Hill, W11 1NN
020 7221 1992
www.booksforcooks.com
Tuesday—Saturday 10am—6pm
Test kitchen: 11.45am—2pm, one sitting; closed for three weeks in August
Tube station: Ladbroke Grove or Notting Hill Gate

Cooking the books isn't always to be frowned upon. The aromas wafting from the kitchen at the back of this culinary bookshop are even more tempting than the appetite-whetting wares that line the shelves. Hungry customers put a selection of recipes from these cookbooks to the test every day.

This Notting Hill institution has become a sort of secret society for foodies. Nurse Heidi Lascelles set up Books for Cooks in 1983. "At that time, British cooking was a standing joke the world over," the shop's website admits. Former resident cooks Annie Bell and Clarissa Dickson Wright soon changed that.

Today, in the open kitchen, the indefatigable chefs produce some of the best value lunches in London. The two- or three-course set menu is always different. Dishes of the day (tweeted to their followers every morning) depend on what's in season. Ingredients are sourced locally from Portobello market, the Moroccan and Portuguese delis on Golborne Road, and The Spice Shop across the street. Organic meat comes from Sheepdrove farm. Lunch might feature lentil and saffron soup, stuffed pork with sage polenta, and upside down pear and ginger pudding. Sweet-toothed locals come for a daily fix of freshly baked cake. Orange meringue, chocolate and Guinness, double ginger, cinnamon swirl with sour cream – all have legions of devotees.

A few stray tourists venture in on Fridays and Saturdays, when Portobello market is in full swing. "Some people come in expecting us to be the bookshop from *Notting Hill*," sighs the manager. The story of the current owners could be mistaken for a cheesy Hollywood script. In 1992, Rosie Kindersley walked into the shop as a customer and walked out an employee. When chef Eric Treuillé sauntered into Books for Cooks a year later, it was *coup de foudre*. The couple took over the business in 2001.

There are compilations of the test kitchen's greatest hits on the till, so you can try to recreate your lunch at home. Demonstrations and tastings are held upstairs, accompanied with wine from Eric's biodynamic vineyard in France. Occasional supper clubs were introduced in summer 2011.

With only a handful of tables, the only drawback is that the food runs out fast – so go early. The cramped, colourful eating area isn't a place to linger; but that's a small price to pay for food that's so affordable and exciting. I'm sure their accounts are above reproach, too.

SPORTING CLUBE DE LONDRES

A secret club for soccer fans

27 Elkstone Road, Notting Hill, W10 5NT
020 8968 3069
www.facebook.com/SportingClubeLondres
charlottemarques@hotmail.co.uk
Wednesday–Thursday 6pm–11pm, Friday 6pm–1.30am, Saturday 1pm–2am,
Sunday 1pm–10.30pm
Tube station: Westbourne Park

At the tail end of Portobello market, Golborne Road is a scruffy jumble of junk shops, Moroccan delis, and Portuguese bakeries that has miraculously escaped gentrification – at least for now. As well as some of the best tagines in London, you'll find the finest *pasteis de nata* (custard tarts) at Lisboa Patisserie, a spartan café permanently abustle

with sweet-toothed Portuguese.

But the real hub of the local Portuguese community is a few blocks away, lodged between a skate park and a council estate on Elkstone Road. A green banner emblazoned with "SCL" is the only clue that this extraordinary restaurant isn't a derelict warehouse. Sporting Clube de Londres opened in 1991 as a social club for the eponymous football team of Portuguese expats. Portugal is a nation of football fanatics. So it's no surprise the walls are lined with football shirts and trophies, and soccer games are shown on giant screens. When there's no match on, Portuguese soaps are played on a loop.

Mid-week the cavernous dining room – all gold chairs and slot machines – is sparsely populated with regulars, who are treated like family by the soft-spoken owner, Rui Daniel Faria Velosa, and his formidable wife Paula. Like any authentic Portuguese restaurant, portions are gigantic and vegetables are an afterthought. Salt cod croquettes, octopus with paprika, and spicy chorizo are followed by platters of *peri peri* chicken, steaming pans of seafood paella, and dangling skewers of succulent meat, the fat dripping onto a heap of home-made chips. It's highly unlikely you'll have the space (or inclination) to sample the fluorescent cakes on display in an illuminated fridge. Molotoff, a cross between meringue pie and crème caramel, is bound to have an explosive effect on your digestive system.

On sunny weekends, there are alfresco barbeques in the yard and bingo sessions every Sunday afternoon. Visit on Friday or Saturday night and the mood is markedly different. The football fans are substituted by boisterous parties of friends and relatives who come for the live music. The entertainment consists of a paunchy crooner performing karaoke versions of Donna Summer, The Gypsy Kings, Elvis and The Police in a heavy Portuguese accent. Medallion men down shots of *aguardente* at the bar, while toddlers and teenagers burn up the dance floor until well past midnight.

NEARBY
Panella

Goldfinger Factory, 13–15 Golborne Road, Portobello, W10 5NY
www.panellalondon.co.uk
Fabulous Sicilian street food made by Giuseppe and Caterina Di Matteo, hiding at the bottom of architectural landmark Trellick Tower.

TSIAKKOS & CHARCOAL

As Greek as it gets

5 Marylands Road, Maida Vale, W9 2DU
020 7286 7896 or text 07398 576102
www.tsiakkos.co.uk
Tuesday—Saturday 7pm—11pm
Tube station: Royal Oak, Warwick Avenue or Maida Vale tube then 10-15 minute walk
Bus: 18

'd often walked past this neighbourhood restaurant and assumed it was closed. A pirate flag and some drab curtains are drawn across the windows, the door is always shut, and the lights seem to be permanently off. Nudge open the door, squeeze past empty beer crates, unpaid bills, a man playing the spoons, and a pair of teenage boys stalking girls on Facebook, and you have arrived at London's finest Cypriot restaurant.

The food is sensational and the mood is Mediterranean holiday. Xen, in beard and baseball cap, mans the barbeque, grilling kebabs and bantering with friends and family members over 20 without breaking sweat. He's been doing this five nights a week, but it's obvious he's still enjoying himself. Xen's parents arrived in London from Cyprus in the early '60s and opened the Mountain Grill cafe on Portobello road, after which Hawkwind named one of their albums. When the owner of his family's favourite Greek restaurant retired, Xen and his wife Elena ("the best cook I ever met") took over. Their three sons, George, Grigoris and Alberto ("named after my wife's dad, my dad, and Alberto Ascari, a racing driver") take turns waiting tables. It's very much a family business – and Xen's regulars are part of the family.

Guests squeeze into the cosy, wood-panelled dining room or the secret garden, clad in bamboo and strung with multicoloured lights. The computer playlist, often hijacked by customers, veers between Barry White, Pulp and David Bowie.

There's a basic wine list, bottles of KEO beer and a menu that never changes. It covers all the Cypriot classics: tarama, humus, haloumi, aromatic pasturma sausages, beetroot spiked with garlic, stewed beans, and Greek salad with a giant chunk of feta. Xen will tell you when he thinks his tarama isn't up to par. If it scores ten out of ten, Xen tapes a cross on the window. Apart from grilled sea bream, mains are meaty. You must order *kleftiko*, a hunk of juicy, crisp-skinned lamb dripping into a heap of clove and cinnamon pilaf, or Xen's signature dish of "slow-burnt pork", marinated in ginger, garlic and lemon squash. "It used to be called slow-cooked pork, but I changed the name after I burnt the Christmas dinner for the team at Books for Cooks" (see page 108).

As the name suggests, you'll leave smelling of charcoal – the lingering aroma of that delicious burnt pork and another bright night at Xen's.

NEARBY
London Shell Co ⑬
The Prince Regent, Sheldon Square, Paddington, W2 6PY
07818 666005
A lovely little barge moored on the Paddington basin serving a menu with a bias towards fresh seafood and fine wines. Step on board for static lunches, Tuesday to Friday. Or book in for an evening or weekend seafood cruise.

OSLO COURT

In the pink

Charlbert Street, St John's Wood, NW8 7EN
020 7722 8795
www.oslocourtrestaurant.co.uk
Monday–Saturday 12:30pm–2:30pm, 7pm–11pm
Closed Sunday and all of August
Tube station: St John's Wood

Student digs aren't what they used to be. Most of the £700,000 flats in Oslo Court are occupied by international students, who enjoy stunning views of Regent's Park and easy access to one of London's most surreal restaurants.

Oslo Court is a 1970s theme park trapped inside a 1930s tower block. The restaurant has no sign, no website, and has never advertised. But on Friday lunchtime, the place is packed with birthday parties, bar mitzvahs, and blue rinses.

After some confusion with our reservation ("Your name is Gaul? Paul? Ah, Hall!"), we were ushered in by a solicitous waiter. The flouncy pink interior is like a paean to the prawn cocktail – a popular fixture on the vast set menu. You can mix and match from dozens of starters, mains and endless specials that never seem to change. Every dish is a throwback: grilled pink grapefruit with brown sugar and sherry, beef Wellington, steak Diane, duckling crisp with cherry sauce, and alarming combinations such as seafood crepe with cheese sauce.

Prices are fixed, but like a Jewish matriarch, they ply you with colossal portions until you're at bursting point. First there are crudités with mayonnaise and warm buttered rolls, a tureen of fish soup, followed by a whole Dover sole and heaps of vegetables. Only the Melba toasts, which taste like leathery slippers, are disappointing.

Spanish brothers Tony and José Sanchez have run the place since 1982 along with their extended family. Our Portuguese waiter's staccato delivery was disconcerting ("Grillfryorpoach? Oilanlemonwhitewineancream-sauceorgarlicbutter? Sautéeboilchipsormash?"), but service is fantastically efficient and comes with lashings of banter. José works the room, introducing himself with the unforgettable line: "My wife is married, but I'm single."

When the dessert waiter minces over, bursting out of his embellished waistcoat, we protest that we are too full. "Come on, Dad!" he says to my younger date. "Just a coupla raspberries? Pieca pavlova to take home?" Neil ("I think it's a stage name – he's Russian," the owner's vivacious daughter Maria Sanchez confides) has been acting the part for over three decades.

Many guests are still wrapping up lunch when the dinner service begins. The whole room bursts into song when a birthday cake is wheeled out. The Oslo Court experience is like being an extra in a *Carry On* film. Although my companion complained that he felt as if he'd "just swallowed a packet of butter," I left feeling buoyant, delighted that such stalwarts can thrive in fashion- and calorie-conscious London. Anyway, you can walk off the butter with a stroll through Regent's Park. Don't forget to take those Melba toasts to feed the ducks.

ALFIES ROOFTOP KITCHEN

Hit the roof

Alfies Antique Market, 13—25 Church Street, Marylebone, NW8 8DT
020 7258 3300
www.rooftopkitchen.co.uk
kamila@rooftopkitchen.co.uk
Tuesday—Saturday 10am—6pm
Tube station: Marylebone or Edgware Road

There are few streets that sum up London's sheer diversity more acutely than Church Street. The Edgware Road end is a blur of cheap fruit and falafel stalls, which give way to elegant antique shops as you approach Lisson Grove. Burqa-clad ladies rummage through heaps of sequined fabrics and gleaming aubergines, while vintage aficionados get their flat white fix from the Indie Coffee cart – the only sign of encroaching gentrification in this unfashionable street market.

In the midst of this frenetic hawking and haggling is Alfies, an Art Deco department store converted into an antiques emporium back in 1976. It was founded by Bennie Gray, who also set up Gray's antiques market in a 19th-century toilet factory in Mayfair. Alfie was the name of his father, "a brilliant jazz musician, but sadly, not a great antique dealer." The pistachio and lemon façade of Alfies looks good enough to eat, but the polished wares inside are even more tempting – provided you have very deep pockets.

If the antiques are out of your league, you can find a bargain at the secret rooftop café. A lovely Brazilian couple, Erick and Kamila, have taken it over and started making fresh-cooked all-day brunch, lunches and afternoon tea. Their eggs Benedict were very fine, and Kamila's home-made cakes looked too yummy to dare try.

But the real draw is the large, hidden terrace, with views across the rooftops to the BT Tower to the east and the glossy office blocks of Paddington Basin to the west. On sunny afternoons, local residents come here with the newspapers to catch some rays. Wheeler-dealers wind each other up over bacon sandwiches and interior designers take a break from maxing out their clients' credit cards downstairs.

NEARBY
George Bar   ⑯
Durrants Hotel, George Street, Marylebone, W1H 5JB
020 7935 8131
www.durrantshotel.co.uk
Durrants, run by the Miller family since 1921, is one of those rare hotels that really feel like home – especially if you happen to live in a posh country house. If you can't afford a room, sink into a leather armchair at the George Bar, a cocoon of gentility that's made for malt whiskies and the Sunday papers. It's like a miniature gentlemen's club with an open fire and judicious bartenders.

THE HERON

Royal regalia and furry fraternising

Norfolk Crescent, Paddington, W2 2DN
020 7724 8463
www.theheronpaddington.com
Daily 11am–11pm
Tube station: Edgware Road

When the Windsor Castle by Edgware Road closed down, its extraordinary collection of regal memorabilia, amassed by former landlord Michael Tierney, needed a new home. And they found it only a couple of streets away. Now the life-size replica of a Foot Guard in a bearskin helmet stands guard in a sentry box outside an unassuming '60s prefab pub down the back of Sussex Gardens. Quick march inside to find a totally unexpected interior lined with Toby jugs and coats of arms, and a ceiling covered in souvenir plates of the royal family. Among the portraits of countless royals are signed photos of soap stars

and celebrities, from George Best to Pierce Brosnan.

The tables are lined with plaques dedicated to former and current regulars. One is "Reserved for Tom and John, celebrating 21 years of being 'civil' to each other." Another is reserved for the Handlebar Club of Great Britain, whose hirsute members gather here on the first Friday of every month, cheerfully slurping cocktail sausages, cucumber sandwiches and pints of bitter between their chops. Most are dressed in "member's regalia" – maroon silk ties and matching sweaters emblazoned with a white moustache. Prospective members must have "a hirsute appendage of the upper lip, with graspable extremities." The other essential qualification is "to be able to drink plenty of beer" and to engage in "furry fraternising," which involves frequent toasts "to the last whisker!" Apparently, members do occasionally engage in charitable stunts, such as finding out how many moustaches fit into a Mini.

Should you wish to air your hair, there's a new little beer garden outside. Or go downstairs to the Thai restaurant to coat your whiskers in spicy coconut milk and stir-fried noodles.

MALAYSIA HALL

Top-secret student canteen

30–34 Queensborough Terrace, Bayswater, W2 3ST
020 798 5126
Daily 8am–10pm
Tube station: Bayswater or Queensway

Malaysia Hall is disconcerting to approach. There's no restaurant sign outside on the residential street – only a laminated notice, explaining that the place is open to Malaysians and authorised personnel only, by order of the High Commission. So I'm a little apprehensive as I descend the steps and poke my head through the door of the basement canteen. I slip into the queue at the counter, hoping the staff will assume the man in front of me is my friend. It seems to work – no one asks for my ID when I choose my dishes from the many on offer, or when I pay only £6 for my melting lamb curry, delicious rich aubergine and fresh pickled vegetable acar, all piled on a plate of steamed rice.

The reason for the security is because it's a government building, and this is really a canteen for newly arrived students, who have halls upstairs. But when I nervously confess that I'm here as a food writer, I am welcomed with a big hug by the owner, who introduces herself as *Kak Ani* – sister Ani. She is originally from Terengganu in the north of the country, where she learned to cook from her mother, who taught home economics. And now she's become a kind of mother to all these young homesick Malaysian students, who get a taste of real home-style cooking and extra-warm hugs.

Of course, *roti canai* (layered paratha-style bread served with curry sauce) is a favourite. The top shelf of the counter holds *nasi lemak* dishes – all-day breakfast Malaysian style – coconut rice with tasty toppings, usually including fish (*ikan*), roasted peanuts and spicy *sambal* sauce. The most prized is the *ikan keli* (catfish), which Ani gigglingly tells me is expensive (£6) because it flies in from Malaysia with its own passport and visa.

At the end of the counter is an array of snack foods – little chicken curry pasties, soft summer rolls, sausage-shaped fish cakes, and plantain fritters which Ani calls "banana batter." Plus little diamond-shaped cakes with a savoury rice layer below and sweet jelly on top. Many of these are so old school that even the Malaysian students don't recognise them.

If you can't find a Malaysian pal to take you here, you can try some of the dishes over in Makan café in Portobello Road, which is run by Ani's husband. But this place is special – and so cheap that you might even offer to buy a student lunch by way of an entry pass.

THE TIROLER HUT

Austrian sing-alongs

27 Westbourne Grove, Bayswater, W2 4UA
020 7727 3981
www.tirolerhut.co.uk
tiroler_reservations@tirolerhut.co.uk
Tuesday–Saturday 6.30pm–1am, Sunday 6.30pm–12.30am
Tube station: Bayswater, Royal Oak or Queensway

The website promises "a lively evening of entertainment including Yodelling, Accordion and the highly original Tyrolean Cow Bell Cabaret." Lively is an understatement. Nothing could prepare you for the nightly performance at this temple to Austrian kitsch.

First, you have to get past the chain-smoking, 70-something doorman, who relishes keeping the weekend crowds at bay. Midweek, you'll have no problem squeezing into the mock-Alpine basement bunker, all gingham curtains, wooden beams, and 1970s posters of blondes on ski slopes. Barmaids in heaving dirndls ply the regulars at the bar with shots of schnapps, while paunchy waiters in lederhosen lubricate the diners with flagons of lager. Josep, a stocky little waiter, can carry six steins in each hand. "I am Leo and dragon, unfortunately not octopus," Josep quips, as he tries to clear the plates of one especially blotto party. This place must be keeping Jagermeister afloat.

A poster of a chimp eating pancakes and drinking a pint sets the mood for the food. The menu – a pork and stodge fest – hasn't changed since Tiroler Hut opened in 1967: there's liver dumpling soup, bratwurst with sauerkraut, schnitzel, or the heart-stopping "*Mir ist alles Wurst*" (mixed fried sausage ensemble). I've never dared to try any of it, but the ladies all seem to favour fondue.

You don't come here for the food; you come for the entertainment. The live music usually starts around 8.30pm. Barricaded in a wooden booth plastered with alpine paraphernalia, a one-man orchestra on a glockenspiel and accordion pounds out a medley that lurches between Elvis, Dolly Parton, Santana and Zorba the Greek. "I'd rather play only Austrian songs, but later on people want a bit of razzmatazz," says Joseph Friedmann, the Hungarian owner and star attraction, whose Austrian wife Christina inspired the Tyrolean theme. His grand finale is a rendition of *Edelweiss* played on a set of cow bells. The whole room sings along, noisily and tunelessly. Friedmann is in his element, although he's been performing the same routine every night for over 40 years. "Not every night," he grins. "We're closed on Mondays."

Surprisingly for somewhere so deeply unfashionable, the Tiroler Hut is a hit with the fashion crowd. A collage of photos commemorates the celebrities who've enjoyed a spot of yodelling, including Claudia Schiffer, Vivienne Westwood, and a naked Juergen Teller face down in a platter of suckling pig. "The internet has helped us a lot," says Friedmann. "Especially as we have Kate Moss on our website – people think she's here every night."

SAFESTAY

Hostel environment

Holland Park, Holland Walk, Kensington, W8 7QU
020 7870 9629
www.safestay.com/london-kensington-holland-park
reception-khp@safestay.com
Monday–Sunday 7am–11pm
Tube station: Holland Park or High Street Kensington

Holland Park might well be the poshest park in all of London. Formerly the grounds of a Jacobean mansion owned by various noble families including one appropriately named Rich, it is now edged by the Design Museum to the south, Lord Leighton's house to the west and a grand row of embassies to the north. It's also the summer residence of Opera Holland Park. In the winter, the peacocks trail their haughty tails in the snow and once I saw black bunny rabbits hop in through the whiteness. Here even the wildlife is tastefully designed.

But slap bang in the middle, hidden behind the opera marquee and the original Jacobean house, is a much more downscale café, where the most expensive meal on offer is the same as the cost of a latte within at least a 3-km radius. It's the canteen of the Safestay hostel, where international backpackers can share a dorm for pennies and save all

Photos by Yogesh Ram

their pounds for a grand tour of Buck Palace. And since they're out all day queuing outside Madame Tussauds, the canteen is usually almost deserted. On a summer's day, you might have to wade knee deep through picnickers on the grand park lawns, but slip round the hedge and into the Safestay courtyard, and it may just be you and a couple of peacocks gazing at your reflections in the elegant fountain pond.

It's definitely not haute-cuisine here, it's cheese-heavy snack foods like toasties, pizzas and lasagne, best suited for twenty-something metabolisms to burn off. You can get some vitamins in the fruit smoothies, and the gluten-free cheese toastie with dressed side salad is pretty darn tasty. They don't serve alcohol, but orange and apple juice are complimentary. In the afternoons, they often give away surplus breakfast pastries. The coffee is the same as the stuff they serve in the official park café, but without the 20-minute queue. If you're bored, there are flat screen TVs inside and a pool table next door. Outside there's ping-pong and a giant shareable hammock. But leave that for the kids. The best thing is just sitting reading or writing at one of the picnic tables on a sunny morning, with the trickle of the fountains and free wifi to accompany your coffee. There are always squirrels and ducks around. The heron which stands stock-still at the water's edge may be cheap plastic, but sometimes a real one flies in, perhaps to see how the other half live. And the answer is: just fine, thank you.

FRANK'S SANDWICH BAR

A pop hit

Addison Bridge Place, West Kensington, W14 8XP
020 7603 4121
www.facebook.com/frankssandwichbar
Monday—Friday 6am—3pm, Saturday 6am—11.45am
Tube/Rail station: Olympia

Leaning against a corner over a railway bridge, in the shadow of the vast Olympia Exhibition space, is a little greasy spoon café. Many pass it by because there are so many big chains around here. The doorway is swamped by a red Coca-Cola sponsored awning, and a few plastic chairs and tables clustered on the edge of a busy road. It's when you wander down the side that you start to think it looks a bit special, maybe even familiar. The building is very narrow with big glass split windows all the way down the side, more like a train carriage than a café – in fact, it's an old converted railway signal box. People sitting at the window are square framed at their seats like a 1970s Polaroid picture. Perhaps the most famous five ever framed here were the members of the band Pulp for the cover of their hit single, "Common People", with Jarvis Cocker at the centre. Though they have some competition: Bryan Ferry and

Adam Ant both used to come here. You might also recognise it from the Lightning Seeds' black and white video for "Change" – the band end up in here as part of a wild night out.

Why such a hit with the pop stars? Maybe it's something to do with being hidden in plain sight. You can't easily see in from the main street, but once inside it's just like the places you remember going to when you weren't a megastar. The interior has that simple elegance of a classic greasy spoon. Plain Formica walls, a galley kitchen with a twin silver-barrelled water urn and a marker board menu. Glass shelves mounted against mirrors, displaying packets of cup-a-soup and brown sauce. The menu is full English breakfast, filled rolls and toasted sandwiches, all prepared fresh on command. The tea is served loose leaf and piping hot from a giant metal teapot. The crockery is proper china.

The eponymous Frank is Frank Cura, who came from Pisa and opened the London café in 1954. Now it's run by his grandson Paul, who first helped out here aged 14. When he got told off at school, he would say, "Don't worry, I'm going to work in my dad's caff." And he did. The film producer Michael Winner also came here as a boy because his dad, who later owned Shepherd's Bush market, had his first property on the corner next door. Michael went back in 1995 and was pleased to report the place was just as he remembered it. And it still is today. Like the Lightning Seeds say, "Don't ever change."

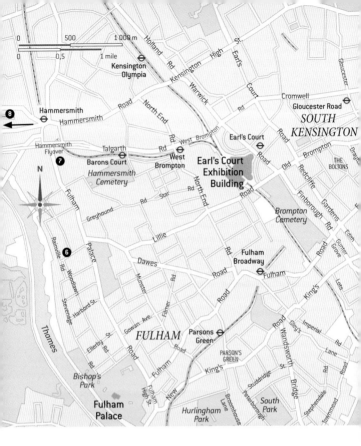

Westminster to Hammersmith

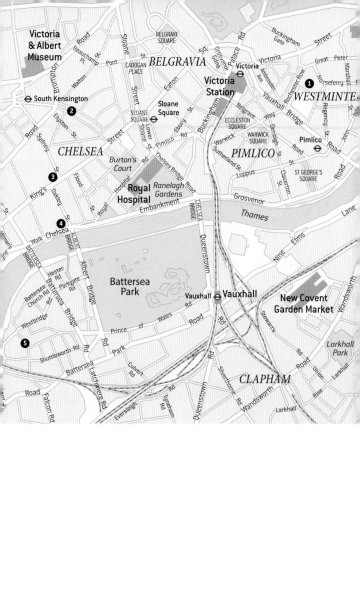

THE VINCENT ROOMS

School dinners

Westminster Kingsway College, 76 Vincent Square, Pimlico, SW1P 2PD
020 7802 8391
www.thevincentrooms.com
Brasserie: Monday–Friday 12pm–2pm and selected evenings 6pm–9pm
Escoffier Room: Monday–Friday 12pm–2pm; closed June & August
Tube station: Victoria

What's a pithivier? I have no idea and my waiter didn't seem to either. "It's a tart sort of thing with mushrooms and some sort of sauce."

Despite an obsession with obscure French culinary terms – Pont Neuf potatoes, *étuvée* of leek, sauce Périgourdine – the food at The Vincent Rooms is less fussy than it sounds. If the retro dining room, with floor-to-ceiling windows overlooking the leafy expanse of Vincent Square, has a school refectory feel that's not surprising: this is a catering school. Launched in 1910 to train chefs for the capital's luxury hotels, Westminster Kingsway College is the alma mater of many of London's chefs, including its most famous alumnus, Jamie Oliver.

The Vincent Rooms is actually two restaurants in one; both serve serious food at knockdown prices, cooked and served by catering and

hospitality students. The flouncy Escoffier Room focuses on haute cuisine, with a seven-course tasting menu, featuring posh ingredients such as foie gras, snails and guinea fowl. Unlike the Escoffier Room, the more low-key Brasserie is occasionally open in the evening.

The menu changes every week and there are several choices for each course. The trainee chefs are clearly being put through their paces: most dishes come with elaborate sauces or wrapped in pastry. Disconcertingly, all the nervous, eager staff seem to be under-age. No wonder they can't open a bottle of wine – they're too young to drink the stuff. The mark-up on wines is very low, a good excuse to get sloshed if the food is hit and miss.

In fact, our supper was consistently good and occasionally brilliant. Poached egg tartlet with leek fricassee, black pudding and bacon crisp looked pretty and tasted pleasingly rich. Cream of white onion and fennel soup with orange mascarpone was an intriguing contrast of refreshing flavours. Pan-fried fillet of sustainable mackerel with potato tartare salad, baby carrots, Portuguese anchovy and chive *beurre blanc* was bright and light, though would have been better warm. My vegetarian friend was delighted with her red onion and chestnut polenta with cauliflower and stilton fritters, served with an endive, mango and Roquefort salad in a pomegranate dressing. Desserts were the only disappointment. Instead of bitter chocolate pudding we got what looked and tasted more like a meatball. At these prices, the occasional dud dish can easily be overlooked.

BARTS

Serviced apartments with hidden benefits

Chelsea Cloisters, Sloane Avenue, Chelsea, SW3 3DW
020 7581 3355
www.barts-london.com
shh@barts-london.com
Sunday–Tuesday 6pm–12am, Wednesday–Friday 6pm–1am, Saturday 2pm–1am
Tube station: South Kensington or Sloane Square

The dark heart of Chelsea is not the sort of place you'd expect to find a clandestine drinking den. Nor indeed is Chelsea Cloisters, a hulking block of serviced apartments rising above the expense account restaurants of Sloane Avenue. Only the building's 1930s architecture gives some clue to the speakeasy that lies within.

Stroll as nonchalantly as you can past the corporate, carpeted reception. On your left is a small black door with an inconspicuous sign. This leads to a booth disconcertingly lined with Mickey Mouse wallpaper and a neon sign for Tattoos & Piercing. Press the buzzer and eventually a flap in the door opens; it's like a gangster movie, only instead of a gun-toting meathead it's a hunky toff who lets you in.

Inspired by L'Esquina in New York – a tequila bar hidden below a taqueria – the venue used to be a bar with a rather seedy reputation

for nocturnal activities. The sultry space is decorated with junk shop curios: cuckoo clocks, vintage signs, and stuffed animal heads. The only concession to the Chelsea location is a trunk filled with wigs, hats and feather boas, catering to the Sloane Rangers' obsession with fancy dress. (Prince Harry would have a field day – and probably has.)

Behind the bar, a fuzzy TV plays old Charlie Chaplin movies. Boys in braces and girls in glad rags dispense shots of absinthe with rum-infused fruit from the Thirst Aid box, or killer concoctions served in top hats and teapots, in line with the Prohibition theme. Signature cocktails have saucy names like Absinthe Minded and Tallulah's Tipple. The Charleston Crumble – rhubarb and pomegranate vodka martini – is especially addictive. As the menu warns: "Two or three of these and you'll be tapping and flapping all night."

The speakeasy soundtrack progresses from '30s swing through to '80s cheese. The crowd is international, but there's a real community spirit. Regulars are given their own key cards and priority booking at weekends, when the small space gets crammed. Even so, many people who live round the corner have yet to discover it.

Illicit pleasures include British comfort food – cheese on toast, sausage rolls, macaroni cheese – and Lucky Strike cigarettes. The cosy backyard is one of the sexiest places for smokers in London. But don't take the "Clothing optional beyond this point" sign seriously. It's cold out there. And if you look up at the winking windows, you'll be reminded that you're in an apartment block.

PHAT PHUC

Happy Buddha Bar

151 Sydney Street, Chelsea, SW3 6NT
020 7351 3843
www.phatphucnoodlebar.co.uk
ppnoodlebar@hotmail.co.uk
Monday—Saturday 11am—6pm
Tube station: South Kensington or Sloane Square, then 10-15-minute walk

I thought Uncle Wrinkle was the most bizarrely named restaurant in London. But that was before I discovered Phat Phuc. This Vietnamese noodle bar is much more appealing than it sounds. Situated beside Chelsea Farmers' Market, the clientele inevitably has a high quotient of Sloane Rangers and bankers' wives. But don't let that put you off either.

Long before London's recent obsession with street food exploded, this outdoor canteen was serving up steaming bowls of noodles to fragrant blondes. Hidden in a courtyard below street level, the ornate food cart strung with paper lanterns was brought all the way from China. But the short Vietnamese menu focuses on *pho* – the cleansing, soothing broth of vegetables and vermicelli flavoured with chicken, beef, or tofu that's served in countless food carts across Vietnam.

Traditionally a breakfast staple, *pho* is a very effective hangover cure (much better than a full English, and with none of the after-effects). Here, it can also provide sustenance on a freezing afternoon of shopping on King's Road. On a summer's evening, sitting at the trestle tables with a bottle of beer, you could almost be on a tropical holiday (although the umbrellas are more likely to protect diners from rain than sun in London's climate). When the bill comes to little more than a tenner, the name makes even more sense: Phat Phuc means 'Happy Buddha' in English.

Half the fun of eating here is sitting at the counter and watching the chef toss the ingredients of your soup into a giant pot, as you inhale the aroma of coriander, a whiff of lime, a splash of soy sauce. You can turn up the heat by dipping into the pretty little bowls of lethal chilli sauce. Besides the *pho*, equally delicious dishes are *bánh cuòn* (summer rolls with prawns or tofu), *bánh xeo* (steamed pancakes with crispy duck and hoisin sauce), and prawn laksa with coconut milk and lemongrass. Portions are so huge that I've never managed to squeeze in a slice of banana cake.

There are photos of the beaming owners with Kevin Bacon and Orlando Bloom beside the till. Apparently, ex Spice Girl Geri Halliwell has also been spotted here. If all those giant vats of noodles start taking their toll on your waistline, you can even buy a Phat Phuc T-shirt.

The cheapest taxi fare in town

Locations: *Chelsea Embankment (near Albert Bridge), SW3; Embankment Place, Charing Cross, WC2; Grosvenor Gardens, Victoria, SW1; Hanover Square, Mayfair, W1; Kensington Park Road, Notting Hill, W11; Kensington Road (north side), South Kensington, W8; Pont Street, Belgravia, SW1; Russell Square (west corner), Bloomsbury, WC1; St George's Square, Pimlico, SW1; Temple Place, Victoria Embankment, WC2; Thurloe Place, South Kensington, SW7; Clifton Gardens, Maida Vale, W9; Wellington Place, St John's Wood, NW8*

London's characteristic black cabs are the direct descendants of the London Hackney Carriage, first licensed by an act of Oliver Cromwell in June 1654. Taxis were built with high roofs so that their illus-

trious clientele didn't have to remove their top hats. However, not all passengers were well bred: in 1694, some lady passengers behaved so badly in a cab near Hyde Park that the authorities banned cabs from the park for the next 230 years.

All of London's cab drivers are required to have "the Knowledge." This exam, introduced in 1865, means cabbies must remember every street within 6 miles of Charing Cross (the official centre of London). This formidable feat can take three years to achieve and only about half of all trainees pass.

Originally, cab drivers weren't allowed to leave their vehicles when parked, so in 1874 the Earl of Shaftesbury set up the Cabmen's Shelter Fund to construct and run roadside huts to provide cabbies with "good and wholesome refreshments at moderate prices." The result was a flourishing of green wooden sheds around the capital. Because the shelters stand directly on a public highway, they could be no bigger than a horse and cart. Even so, they still manage to squeeze in a working kitchen and space for over ten men. The philanthropists who set up the shelters were typically high-minded Victorians: gambling, drinking, swearing and talking politics were strictly forbidden. The original intention in getting the cabmen into the shelters was not only to feed them, but also to keep them out of the pub.

There were originally 61 of these shelters, but numbers have dwindled to 13. The few remaining sheds, often in some of the poshest

parts of London, are now listed buildings. Thankfully, they still thrive as a place for colleagues to meet and eat. Only cabbies are allowed to sit inside, but anyone can get a take-away – "bacon roll, brown sauce, tea, three sugars, thanks love" – through the serving hatch. The menu is generally basic fare such as sausage rolls and ham and cheese sandwiches, although some shelters will knock up a full English breakfast. Prices are dirt-cheap, but sweet-toothed patrons might be penalised: "Please note if you would like 4-5-6 sugars in your tea or coffee, you will be charged 5p extra."

LE QUECUMBAR

Gypsy Queen

42 —44 Battersea High Street, SW11 3HX
020 7787 2227
www.quecumbar.co.uk
info@quecumbar.co.uk
Monday—Thursday 7pm—12am, Friday—Sunday 6pm—12am; closed Wednesdays
Live music 8pm—11pm; no entry after 10.30pm
Rail station: Clapham Junction then 15-minute walk
Buses: 170, 319

Battersea High Street is a confusingly named road – no branches of Sainsbury's, Starbucks or even a Snappy Snaps. There's a cluster of local shops at the south end, but it quickly becomes a quiet residential back street. You almost give up hope as you pass under the bridge and see only housing estates ahead. But then you spot the smiling mustachio'd face of Django Reinhardt and you know you've found something special.

Step inside and you're transported to 1930s Paris. Tobacco yellow walls, tables skirted in terracotta cloth and dark wooden curved chairs. Everything is wreathed in greenery and twinkling fairy lights, creating a magical ambience. In the corners are two small stages: on one a baby grand piano graced by a pink flamingo feathered lamp, on the other a double bass just waiting to be seized and spun. When the evening's entertainment begins, one of these stages will be crammed with musicians and the room will be jumping with Gypsy Swing sounds.

Set up in 2003 by Django Reinhardt devotee Sylvia Rushbrooke on the 50th anniversary of her musical hero's death, this is the only dedicated Gypsy Swing venue in the world – and so musicians come from all around the globe to play in the back streets of Battersea.

From the time that an early boyfriend first played her one of his dad's Django records, Sylvia was hooked on the music of this Belgian-born Sinti Gypsy guitarist, composer and band leader. He and his band, the Quintette du Hot Club de France, pretty much invented European jazz by mixing traditional Gypsy music with American jazz. The result is so bouncy and vibrant, it instantly fills the room with a joyous energy, forcing you to jig along, even if you've had one of Le Q's "hearty not haughty" dinners. I was sort of hoping for some Gypsy dishes on the menu but baked hedgehog was nowhere to be found. It's mainly French brasserie classics like *Savoie tartiflette* and *coq au vin*. There's a magical little tropical garden out the back where you can smoke your Gauloises or just take a rest from all the jigging.

Bigger and overseas acts are ticketed in advance on Sundays and Mondays, but on most nights, arrive before 8pm – or any time Tuesday

– and entry is free. It's the kind of place where you can go dressed up for a really special night out, or just turn up in your jeans and have an accidentally great Tuesday evening. I shall definitely be back – this hot club is cool as a quecumbar.

MES AMIS

A feast for all senses

1 Rainville Road, Hammersmith, W6 9HA
020 7385 5155
Monday–Saturday 7pm–11.30pm
Tube station: Hammersmith then 15-minute walk
Buses: 295, 211, 190, 220

Unless you happen to live locally or get lost looking for The River Café down the road, you won't stumble upon this little Lebanese local. The brilliantly bizarre interior looks more Mexican than Middle Eastern: stained-glass lanterns dangle from hand-painted ceilings suspended with parasols. Musical instruments, masks, paintings and plants jostle for wall space. Collections of cruet sets, teapots and stuffed toys are crammed onto every surface. Patterned carpets clash with chairs upholstered in loud florals. The fireplace is painted in primary colours. Tables are laid with spotted napkins, brocade tablecloths and fake bouquets. Even the toilet paper is printed with butterflies. To get to the psychedelic loos, you have to squeeze through a TV lounge lined with DVDs and old Elvis LPs.

This inspired interior is the handiwork of James Ilyas, a Syrian who arrived in Britain aged 11. The corner site was a boarded-up ruin when he moved in 20 years ago. Night after night, Ilyas presides over proceedings from his tiny open kitchen in the centre of the room. Dressed to kill in a glittery sweater, leather cap and bushy moustache, he looks like an ageing Village People impersonator. Ilyas works calmly, picking fresh ingredients from bowls on the kitchen counter. A pair of stuffed bunnies stands guard atop two towering jars of pickles.

The short bill of fare offers just three starters and seven main courses. "The menu reads like the corner kebab shop. You'd never expect food of this quality," said my companion, as we dunked and chomped our way through a spread of mezze. Smoky *baba ganoush*, delicately spiced meat samosas, zingy tabouleh and juicy kofte all disappeared quickly. Meaty mains are huge. Chicken shish kebab is drizzled in tahini sauce and served on a fragrant mound of chickpea, courgette and mushroom couscous. A minced lamb patty in yoghurt and tomato sauce garnished with blood orange and lime looks as good as it tastes. There's no dessert menu but a selection of bite-sized baklava appears on the house.

Our waitress Regina, a poised, gracious blonde, has worked here since the restaurant opened. With only a handful of tables, she knows most of her guests by name. "We've become friends with so many of our customers over the years," says Ilyas, who often makes special dishes for regulars. It's no accident that he called his deliciously eccentric establishment Mes Amis.

THE VILLAGE

Somali stir-up

95 Fulham Palace Road, Hammersmith, W6 8JA
020 8741 7453
www.somalirestaurant.co.uk
info@somalirestaurant.co.uk
Monday–Thursday 12pm–11pm
Tube station: Hammersmith

Despite the grand history of Somali seafarers and lascars settling in Britain's ports, there are currently only a handful of Somali restaurants in London, and The Village might be the hardest to spot. A narrow green doorway squished into the cluttered strip south of the Hammersmith roundabout. Enter and it looks like there's only one table by the reception desk. But head downstairs and you'll find a little basement restaurant, simply decorated in red and white with a few Somali handicrafts around, including a wooden neck rest which allows the user to sleep without messing up their elaborate hairdo. This is a humble place, there's no alcohol licence and don't expect fine dining. But it's a major meeting point for the Somali community: they come from all over London to have a taste of home cooking, or often to introduce it to their friends. Even British Somali hero Mo Farah has dropped by. Somali culture prides itself on generosity, so expect a warm welcome, cheap prices and huge portions. Plus the restaurant is co-owned by the staff so they are all invested in making you feel content.

Located on the most easterly point of mainland Africa, Somalia is lapped by the Arabian Sea and Indian Ocean and was fought over by European colonial powers who all wanted control of the strategically positioned ports. So Somali cuisine reflects this battle of influences. In the starters you will find samosas and falafels, in the mains there's slow-cooked lamb shank, tortellini, and Arabic-style grilled chicken and fish. All of these can be accompanied by African fave soft sorghum (*soor* or *masago*), Indian-style rice, Italian spaghetti (*baasto*) in a tomato and coconut sauce – or good old British mashed potato. Often you'll get a ladleful of a green sauce over the top – *sugu agar* – which looks a lot like the liquor you get in pie and mash shops, but is made from coriander and spinach. With a hot coconut sambal on the side, it's quite a mix!

There is also a bit of a menu battle between coastal pescatarians and mainland carnivores, who will ask, "Why eat fish when you can have camel?" (I was slightly disappointed not to find any camel to try, reputedly the king of meats). If you (amazingly) have room for dessert, you will find boiled date cake and tiramisu. And if all this clash of cultures leaves you considering 40 winks on the neck rest, there's a beautiful post-prandial walk along the Thames just a street away. You just need to work out whether to say *choukran, merci, grazie* or thank you.

LOWICZANKA

Dumplings on the dance floor

238–246 King Street, Hammersmith, W6 0RF
020 8741 3225
www.lowiczankarestaurant.com
contact@lowiczankarestaurant.com
Tuesday–Friday 12.30pm–3pm and 6.30pm–9pm, Saturday 12.30pm–3pm
and 6.30pm–12am, Sunday 12.30pm–9pm
Tube station: Ravenscourt Park or 15-minute walk from Hammersmith
Bus: 27

I f you happen to love Boney M and schnitzels, Lowiczanka is the only place to be on a Saturday night. It is buried deep within the concrete bunker that is the Polish Social and Cultural Association (POSK), a hunk of Soviet-era brutalism that is the heart of London's Polish community. The POSK HQ contains a Joseph Conrad library, a jazz bar in the basement, and a member's club on the fourth floor. Anyone brave enough can visit the first-floor restaurant, Lowiczanka, but we were the only non-Poles on a Saturday night.

On first impression, we seemed to have wandered into a dinner dance on a dodgy cruise. There were gilt-edged mirrors, potted palms and dolled-up blondes. Once the Fantasy Band (a dour quartet of porky Poles) started up, it was more like we'd gatecrashed a wedding in Lodz. As the synthesised strains of Chris Rea belted out, there was a middle-aged surge towards the dance floor. By midnight, even the glamorous septuagenarians in skin-tight leopard-skin and fur stoles at the next table were getting down to a medley of '70s disco, Polish pop and frenetic fiddling. The band segued breathlessly from *My Bonny Lies over the Ocean* to *Guantanamera*. The drummer even pulled off a plausible Louis Armstrong impersonation, with just a trace of a Polish accent. "This must be the Polish version of 'I will survive,'" said one of my companions, as the crowd went wild.

The menu valiantly keeps up the 1970s theme. There are pancakes, sausages and schnitzels large enough to feed a family. Despite the disquieting images of fluorescent canapés on the restaurant's website, the food is surprisingly good. We slurped down cabbage borscht with sausage and clear beetroot broth – the perfect stomach-liner and liver-cleanser before we got stuck into the vodka. Shredded carrot, beetroot and cabbage accompanied hefty portions of potato rosti slathered with goulash and a lucky dip of *pierogi* stuffed with cream cheese and potato, sauerkraut and mushroom. The clear winner was roast goose in cherry sauce that fell off the fork and melted in the mouth. Dense poppy seed strudel came with a garnish of tinned peaches. How the other patrons managed to scoff such hearty food and then bounce around the dance floor was beyond me.

The only sour note wasn't the lashings of sour cream. It was the £60 unaccountably added to our bill. Our apologetic waitress blamed "the calculator," but I think the manager assumed we'd had too many vodka shots to notice.

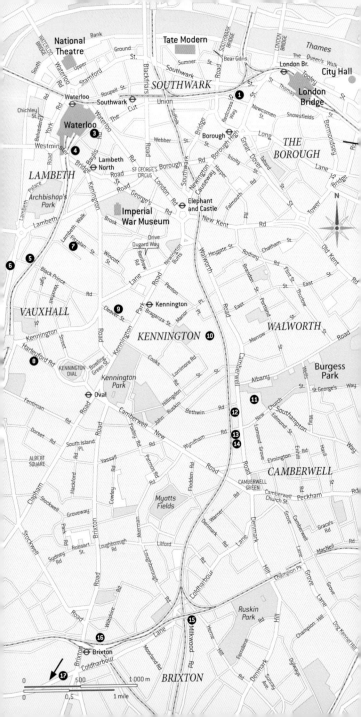

South Bank to Brixton

THE BOOT & FLOGGER

Vintage wines and punchable nuns

10–20 Redcross Way, Borough, SE1 1TA
020 7407 1184
www.davy.co.uk
bootandflogger@davy.co.uk
Monday 11am–10pm, Tuesday–Saturday 11am–11pm, Sunday 12pm–6pm
Tube station: Borough or London Bridge

This is not an S&M club; it's a wine bar. The suggestive name refers to an old corking device: the bottle was steadied inside a leather "boot" while the cork was "flogged" into place using a wooden mallet.

With its wood-panelled walls and wing-backed leather armchairs, The Boot and Flogger has the snug ambience of a gentlemen's club. Antique prints, wig boxes, and dusty bottles of vintage port decorate the warren of rooms. The decor may look Dickensian, but in fact it dates to 1965. Housed in a converted smokehouse, the bar was founded by the Davy family, a dynasty of wine merchants and innkeepers since 1870. Many of the customers have been coming since it opened.

The giant barrels behind the bar are no longer in use, but house champagne is served in silver tankards, which keep the fizz colder for longer. There's a tantalising list of special wines and a cracking selection of sherry, port and Madeira.

The old boys soak up the booze with hearty plates of seafood, game or gammon, served with verve by motherly waitresses. More port is consumed with a generous cheese plate or Bramdean pudding, a rich concoction of crushed biscuits, raisins, cream, custard and lashings of sherry.

Despite the smoking ban, cigars are available for sale. Smokers retire to the courtyard, where the stables date from the building's previous life as a fire station. In those days, fire engines were horse-drawn, as were taxis, as an old sign inside attests: "New post chaises and able horses at the shortest notice."

As you totter out into the Southwark night, pay your respects at the Cross Bones graveyard across the road. This unhallowed patch of wasteland contains the bodies of over 15,000 paupers and prostitutes, more commonly known as Winchester Geese, buttered buns, or punchable nuns. The graveyard gates are cloaked in colourful ribbons and totems; a vigil for the outcast is held at 7pm on the 23rd of each month.

NEARBY
The Doodle Bar　　　　　　　　　　　　　　　②

60 Druid Street, SE1 2EZ
020 7403 3222
www.thedoodlebar.com

The Doodle Bar has moved from Battersea to an archway halfway between London Bridge and Bermondsey. Decorate the chalkboard walls with your doodles, drink doodle beer brewed specially in Belgium, and doodle around the creative events in "TestBed1", the raw cavernous space behind which they are planning all sorts of artistic experiments, performances and secret clubs.

MARIE'S CAFÉ

Sweet and sour bacon and eggs

90 Lower Marsh, Waterloo, SE1 7AB
020 7928 1050
www.mariescafe.co.uk
Monday—Friday 7am—10.30pm, Saturday 7am—4pm and 5pm—10.30pm
Tube station: Waterloo, Southwark or Lambeth North

Although it's full of market traders and cab drivers on a midweek morning, this isn't your average greasy spoon. The chilli sauce on the counter alongside the ketchup and brown sauce is the first clue. The blackboard menu may be all liver and onions, steak and kidney pie, eggs bacon chips and beans, but pinned on scraps of paper around the nicotine-coloured room are less traditional "daily specials" – sweet and sour prawns, fish ball soup, lychees and ice cream.

Marie's Café may look like the real deal, from the vintage signage to the original grease-stained counter, but its Italian namesake retired 25 years ago. A team of friendly Thais moved in. They didn't change much, apart from the addition of a few peeling posters from Thailand's tourist board circa 1980. After mastering the art of a good fry-up, the new owners gradually added a few Thai specialities to the menu. Now Marie's becomes a fully-fledged Thai restaurant after 5.30pm.

The menu has been shortened and the typos fixed (farewell oh crispy filler of cod and homedal chilli sauce). Fish cakes in chilli and peanut sauce are pleasingly squeaky. Salads laced with fresh chillies will bring tears to your eyes, but the curries are fairly mild. Green chicken curry and chicken penang both stand out, and the pad Thai is delicious. The sweet waitresses are always smiling (especially when they have no idea what you're saying) and you can bring your own booze.

NEARBY
Scooter Caffe ④
132 Lower Marsh, SE1 7AB
020 7620 1421

If the rough-and-ready atmosphere at Marie's doesn't cut it, order a takeaway and eat it at this idiosyncratic bar down the road. There's no sign outside: to find it, look for the vintage scooter in the window and the red neon sign proclaiming BAR among the second-hand shops and food stalls of Lower Marsh. Formerly a Vespa garage with a tiny espresso bar, this ramshackle joint has morphed into a cosy café-bar. The 1957 Faema coffee machine pumps out phenomenal hot chocolate and cappuccino. They roast their own coffee, and bake their own cakes at the nearby Cable Bakery. The resident cat Bob is actually a girl who was born behind the bar.

RAGGED CANTEEN

Cultured vegetarian

Beaconsfield, Newport Street, Vauxhall, SE11 6AY
020 7758 6465
www.beaconsfield.ltd.uk/cafe
theraggedcanteenkitchen@gmail.com
Monday–Sunday 11am–5pm
Tube station: Vauxhall, Lambeth North or Kennington

U nless you're a fan of Portuguese restaurants and/or gay clubs, you might never have ventured into Vauxhall. Although only moments from the Thames and a short stroll from Parliament, this scruffy little patch of South London is marooned between so many ring roads that it's often overlooked. Fortunately, this has allowed Beaconsfield, an artist collective set up in 1995, to survive.

The tall, walled building sits incongruously among the mechanics who have set up shop in the railway arches lining Newport Street. It opened in 1851 as Lambeth Ragged School, a free school-cum-soup kitchen for impoverished children. Only the girls' wing has survived, as two-thirds of the school was knocked down to make way for the South Western Railway at the turn of the 20th century. Later, the fire brigade used it as a rehearsal room for their brass band. During the Blitz, the windows facing Parliament were blacked out.

The exploding logo outside is a sign of what's in store: a gallery that blows up people's preconceptions. Ring the buzzer and it's a welcome surprise to find punters chowing down on vegetarian food in a yard that's hidden behind the high brick wall.

Inside the café, an informal space with flagstone floors and whitewashed walls, folksy music burbles above the satisfying thrum of spirited conversation. Daily specials – like felafel burgers with sweet potato wedges, squash, ricotta and sage ravioli, spicy peanut soup – are chalked up on a blackboard. They bake their own bread and cakes, and there's always a vegan and gluten-free option. At weekends they serve all-day brunches. Everything is produced in the tiny open kitchen by chef Tim Laskey, whose eclectic recipes are "begged, borrowed and stolen from all over the place." "It's quite rough and ready," he cheerily admits. "We didn't even have an oven for the first year and a half." The herb garden on the roof supplies some ingredients; the rest are as locally sourced as possible.

The clients are a mixed bag of local residents, artists, mums and workers. "Well, the more adventurous workers who are willing to brave the arts and cross the threshold of strangeness," smiles David Crawforth, who co-founded Beaconsfield. "The art is often challenging and political."

Certainly, you needed a strong stomach to watch chilling footage of the civilian victims of drone strikes in Waziristan in the gallery upstairs. Thankfully, I soon recovered my appetite with a delicious slice of Victoria sponge.

NEARBY

Tamesis dock ⑥

Albert Embankment, Vauxhall, SE1 7TP
020 7582 1066
www.tdock.co.uk

There's live ukulele-playing on Wednesday nights at this Dutch barge moored between Lambeth and Vauxhall Bridges. The look is hippy-trippy, but the view from the deck is sensational.

THE OXYMORON

Random order

Royal Oak, 78 Fitzalan Street, Kennington, SE11 6QU
07515 878976
www.facebook.com/The-Oxymoron-818445384860869
asilhendry@gmail.com
Monday—Friday 3pm—11.30pm, Saturday and Sunday 2.30pm—11.30pm
Tube station: Kennington

Photos by Rachel Megawhat

The Oxymoron is well named. It's the opposite of what you'd expect from a freehouse pub. It's an outlandish local with a festively tranquil vibe. It is barely 20 minutes' walk from the centre of town, but no one can find it. Even locals are quietly shocked to discover it's there. Back in September 2009, it was an old boozer that was not really worth travelling any distance for. But then local jewellery craftworkers Lisa Hendry and William Prophet took it over and started to polish up this rough diamond.

Cheerful pessimist Lisa first met retiring extrovert William at a jewellery trade show where he'd flashed open his coat to display his entire stall hanging in the lining. Despite having no publican experience or any real plan, they acquired the dingy pub and started to gut it themselves. Their artist friend David Scott pushed them on with a vision of a wonderful gastro pub. William worked out how to build and fix literally everything. And Lisa started to decorate – acquiring things from car boot sales and flea markets. Dark corners and high shelves were filled with random plates, tins, clocks, pieces of brass and copper. William found a load of ornate gilded wood in a skip, so Lisa pinned it above the bar and started to cover it with dismembered dolls, plastic ducks, shockheaded trolls and bright coloured baubles – it's as if someone has raided a toddler's toybox. Sprouting from the walls of the little back garden are totem poles made of swans, badgers and Buddha heads. Twisted through everything are yards and yards of colourful fairy lights, cheerfully glowing but never quite revealing the vast and fabulous array of magical-realist clutter. William's sister Linda joined them behind the bar and has been there every day since – countering his craziness with her loyal stability. They never quite figured the gastro bit, but people can use the kitchen themselves for parties or pop-up events, when they can cook full dinners or just reheat food. They have bands playing and open mike nights. They get late licences for parties. And an eclectic mix of people come from far and near. Sometimes the pub is rammed with partiers;

sometimes it's just a few locals and their dogs. They shouldn't stay open but they do. Make sure you visit – the Oxymoron is a minor miracle.

BONNINGTON CAFÉ

An anarchic anachronism

11 Vauxhall Grove, Vauxhall, SW8 1TD
www.bonningtoncafe.co.uk
Cooks' telephone numbers on the website
Daily 12pm–5pm and 6.30pm–10.30pm
Tube station: Vauxhall

"**Y**ou don't come here for the food, you come to get progressively drunk and enjoy the atmosphere," my companion warned me as we sat down. This vegetarian cooperative probably won't dispel carnivores' preconceptions about vegetarian food as bland stodge that makes you fart. But the cosy, candlelit atmosphere really is special.

Like the other Victorian houses on Bonnington Square, condemned to demolition after being bombed during the Second World War, this one was taken over by squatters in the early '80s. Initially the café was a communal kitchen, because the squats didn't have gas, electricity or water. People paid whatever they could afford. Ingredients were leftovers from New Covent Garden market nearby.

Thirty years on, many of the properties (now worth over £1 million) are privately owned; the rest are run by low-rent housing associations. "It's a weird mix of old hippies and the super-posh, but they all come to the café," says Rachel Ortas, an illustrator who has been cooking here for over a decade. Still collectively run, the bohemian café hasn't changed with the times. There are purple walls, flowery plastic tablecloths and maps plastered on the ceiling. Prices are deliberately kept low, and are even cheaper at lunchtime.

With a different amateur cook every night, the cuisine and quality vary. There are about ten regular cooks and a waiting list of wannabe chefs from all over the world, so you might get a Malaysian, Italian, or even a medieval menu. My companion advised me to avoid the raw vegan supper. "After trying the 'zucchini linguini', I didn't come back for a year."

Tonight, there were just two choices per course. I chose "comfy chowder soup" (discomfortingly served cold) and gratin dauphinoise (a gloopy mass of overcooked potato drenched in tomato sauce). My companion struggled with a "Spanish platter" – a dry veggie burger served with rice and beans. I couldn't see where Spain came into the equation. A squidgy chocolate tart "didn't taste of chocolate."

Service can be chaotic: "If someone forgets it's their night to cook, then the café is shut," proclaims the café's manifesto. They don't bother with napkins. It's not just bring your own booze, it's bring your own salt. But our gripes dissolved when two French waitresses with ukuleles emerged from the kitchen to entertain us with a "*chanson classique*." Authentic and ad hoc, it's amazing that this idealistic relic has survived. You leave with a warm, fuzzy glow, even if you're farting all the way home.

PRINCE OF WALES

Fannying around

Cleaver Square, Kennington, SE11 4EA
020 7735 9916
www.princeofwaleskennington.co.uk
powkennington@shepherdneame.co.uk
Monday–Saturday 12pm–11pm, Sunday and Bank Holidays 12pm–10.30pm
Tube station: Kennington or Oval
Buses: 12, 35, 40, 45, 68, 133

Photo by Colin Taylor

The Prince of Wales stands in a pretty Georgian square hidden in the heart of Kennington. The area itself is a bit of a secret, kept hush hush by politicians who can nip across the bridge for a late vote at Westminster and be home in time for last orders. And so this lovely village-style pub, owned by the Shepherd Neame Brewery, is pretty good for political star spotting. But it's a different sort of sport which wins it the extra votes.

Cleaver Square, named after the 18th-century landowner Mary Cleaver, is coated in loose gravel, making it perfect for a game of pétanque – aka boules – one of the few games you can play in the sunshine with a glass of wine in your hand. This is where the London Pétanque Club used to hold their competitions, though the square got so packed they have rolled on to the more spacious Vauxhall Pleasure Gardens, and are now based at the lovely Tea House Theatre (which is actually a pub serving fine wine and cakes).

So while the LPC support the campaign for pétanque to become an Olympic sport, they've left Cleaver Square free for friendly matches and complete amateurs. For a mere £10 deposit, the Prince of Wales staff will lend you a set of heavy metal boules, along with a coche, short for cochonnet (little pig), the little wooden ball. Work in teams of two or three, draw a circle in the gravel and throw the coche 6–10 metres out from it. Then aim to get your boules closest to the coche, or alternatively shoot to knock your opponents' balls away. If your team's ball is on point (closest to the coche), you can stand around and drink until you're knocked off your perch. Queue much pondering, pacing, muttering and measuring (don't forget to bring a measuring tape). First to thirteen points wins. If you lose thirteen nil, that's called being fannied. "Tu es fanny!", they cry, and then you must kiss the bottom of a girl named Fanny. Or buy the next round, whichever is soonest …

It's a game you can play all year round – though if the snow is very deep you might want to go for an inside piste like the one at Baranis (see page 68). You might have to take a day off for the occasional street party, and the Kennington village fête in May. But then you get to watch Morris dancers fannying around and that's almost as entertaining.

NEARBY

The Beehive ⑩

62 Carter Street, West Walworth, SE17 3EW
020 7703 4992
www.thebeehivepub.london

Fifteen minutes east of here is The Beehive, hidden so deep in the heart of residential Walworth that only the locals know it's there. One of the few buildings in the area to survive the blitz, it's now a big pub with a lovely sunny terrace and a beer garden cloaked in giant sunbrellas.

FOWLDS CAFÉ

Fully restored

3 Addington Square, Camberwell, SE5 7JZ
020 3417 4500
fowldscafe.com
info@fowldscafe.com
Monday–Friday 7.30am–5pm, Saturday 8.30am–5pm, Sunday 9.30am– 4pm
Tube station: Elephant & Castle
Buses: 148, 35, 171, 68, 12, 40, 45

Fowlds tiny café is just off the Walworth Road, at the point where Walworth meets Camberwell. If you thought the area was all hairdressers, chicken shops and branches of Cash Converters, you haven't been into Addington Square. It's full of beautifully designed grand Georgian and Victorian houses, oxbowing round an outcrop of Burgess Park – a vast green stretch which hides a blue tiled Islamic palm tree oasis at its centre.

Addington Square has known its rougher times. In the 1960s the Richardson gang, rivals of the Krays, had a private club there where they threw wild parties, kept a couple of bears, and held kangaroo courts where Mad Frankie Fraser practised unskilled dentistry on the guilty.

Thirty years later, when Jack Wilkinson moved into the square, there was nowhere nearby to get a decent coffee and you had to go all the way to Borough Market to buy good bread. Jack, who was doing a Masters in Product Design, loved the Victorian upholstery workshop he walked past each day. His thesis was on complementary businesses and there was something about furniture restoration and coffee which seemed symbiotic. Both warm and cosy, both craft businesses. You sit on a sofa to drink coffee, don't you?

Bob Fowlds – whose grandfather had started the upholstery business in 1870, moving to the square in 1926 – wasn't so sure about the collaboration. But after a few months' persistence, Jack finally persuaded Bob to give up his small front display room. Local residents, whose names are on a plaque by the door, helped fund the venture. Jack's design – he did everything from the lampshades to the counter tiles – managed to fit a counter and 14 (very friendly) customers inside, with another 12 under the awning outside. As well as great coffees and bread from the Little Bread Pedlar, talented local chef Hannah Cole rustles up delicious breakfasts, sandwiches, soups, salads and cakes.

Fowlds is great on a sunny morning – and can get quite packed on Sundays, when the park runners gather there. Just before Christmas, Bob lets Jack convert his workshop into the "Fowlds Feasts" supper club, with a banqueting table and fairy lights stretching down through the workshop and out into the back of the Fowlds furniture delivery van. It has definitely restored the square to its full glory. And sometimes the customers even bring their furniture for similar treatment.

PASHA

Magic carpet

Pasha Hotel, 158 Camberwell Road, Camberwell, SE5 0EE
020 7871 9963
www.pasharestaurants.co.uk
eat@pasharestaurants.co.uk
Saturday and Sunday 1pm—11pm , Monday—Thursday 6pm—12am
Tube station: Elephant & Castle then 15-minute walk
Buses: 148, 12, 35, 45

Walworth Road wilfully refuses to smarten up. Running into Camberwell Road, it's one long blur of Chinese takeaways, evangelical churches, nail parlours and fried chicken shops. I can't imagine why any traveller would choose to stay here, but the plucky Kyrgyz owners of Pasha Hotel beg to differ.

Indeed they have recently refurbished the place, which is now a hotel and spa, featuring London's only private hammam. The colourful restaurant is still hidden at the end of a long corridor.

Seating is mainly on carpeted divans scattered with cushions (take my advice: don't wear a short skirt). Central Asian pop is punctuated by the intermittent rattle of a train, which seems to run right through the restaurant. There is a dance floor for belly dancing on Fridays and live music on Saturday evenings.

Our endearingly cheerful waitress brought humus and fluffy flatbread while we dithered over the multi-ethnic menu. Inspired by the Silk Road, it's a medley of dishes from Kyrgyzstan, Kazakhstan and Turkmenistan, from *imam bayildi* to pickled herring. There's Georgian wine and Russian beer. Main courses focus on meat and heavy carbs – kebabs, noodles, dumplings. Some dishes, such as lamb's tongue and chicken roulade with pickles, are only for the brave.

Our starters fell flat. *Olivie* (a salad of boiled beef, potato and egg mayonnaise) "tastes like school dinners," my companion sniffed. My stuffed vine leaves were mushy and bland. We perked up when the main courses arrived. Beef and onion *manti* (dumplings) with sour cream and kick-ass tomato sauce are made to order but were worth the wait. *Lagman* turned out to be "spag bol Krygyz style" – hand-made noodles with strips of spicy beef. *Plov*, spicy carrot pilaf with baked lamb, was much better than it sounded. *Chack chack*, billed as "the lightest of pastry desserts", was anything but light – "more like refried bits of *jalebi*." But with such gracious service, amazingly low prices and remarkable surroundings, I'll be back. I might even brave the belly dancer.

ZERET KITCHEN

What wot!

216 Camberwell Road, Camberwell, SE5 0ED
020 7701 8587
www.zeretkitchen.com
Monday–Thursday 1pm–10.30pm, Friday and Saturday 1pm–11.30pm,
Sunday 1pm–9.30pm
Buses: 12, 35, 40, 45, 148, 171, 176, 468

Zeret Kitchen is nestled into a little grey square on the Castle Mead estate off the Walworth Road, dwarfed by a huge tower block and hidden behind a busy bus stop and blocks of bicycle racks. Tafe Belayneh and her husband Berhanu first opened a tiny daytime caff here in 2004, back when the locals didn't trust anything more exotic than a

bit of mustard on their sausage sandwich. Tentatively, Tafe introduced them to her home-cooked Ethiopian food. It took a while, but delicious flavours, super-cheap prices and friendly service gradually persuaded enough customers for the couple to transform it into a full Ethiopian restaurant and expand into a second room.

What's interesting is that Ethiopian food is nowadays becoming quite sought-after as it hits all the current trends for gluten-free, vegan, low-fat and fermented. The Ethiopian Orthodox Church has a 3,000-year-old tradition of no animal or dairy products on Wednesdays, Fridays or during Lent, so the cuisine features lots of delicious vegan dishes. Food is served on naturally fermented sourdough pancakes called *injera*, made partially or entirely from gluten-free *teff* flour and cooked on big iron hot plates with hardly any oil. Your dinner will arrive hidden under a woven straw hat, or *mosop*, which is lifted theatrically to reveal your giant pancake platter (best ensure everyone you're dining with is comfortable with sharing). You tear off a bit of your side of the pancake base and use it to pinch a mouthful of the *wots* (curries), *tibs* (grilled marinated meats) and salads that are daubed prettily on top. Everything in the house special I tried was tasty but the vegan dishes were outstanding, especially the *shiro wot* – a thick sauce made of spicy roasted powdered chickpeas, and the *defin misr alecha* – a green lentil curry spiced with mustard and ginger.

In the drinks menu you'll find Ethiopian Castel beer and – even more special – freshly made home-brewed honey wine. And after dinner, if no one else has ordered it, try the aromatic coffee ceremony: fresh green beans are roasted over charcoal, brewed at your table and then the thick black coffee is poured from a great height into little cups and served with a side order of fresh popped corn and a chunk of smouldering frankincense – filling the whole restaurant with an intoxicating mix of perfumes.

NEARBY

Margaret's Cakes of Distinction (14)

224 Camberwell Road, Camberwell, SE5 0ED
020 7701 1940
www.margaretscakesofdistinction.co.uk
Cakes must be ordered in advance

As you head back out into the square, don't forget to peer into the next-door window of Margaret's Cakes of Distinction, where you can pre-order amazing English and West Indian celebration cakes, iced and decorated with the most elaborate handmade sugar sculptures.

WHIRLED CINEMA

Up the Junction

259–260 Hardess Street, Brixton, SE24 OHN
020 7737 6153
www.whirledcinema.com
rob@whirledcinema.com
Monday–Wednesday: doors open 7pm, screenings 8pm; Sunday: doors open
5pm, screenings 6pm
Rail station: Loughborough Junction
Buses: 35, 45, 345, P4

Brixton has become cool again, since a flurry of top-notch food stalls set up shop in the covered market. Now you can feast on pad Thai, gourmet burgers or biodynamic salads before a screening at the wonderful Ritzy Cinema. It's all jerk chicken rather than satay skewers around Loughborough Junction, a scruffy patch on the rough outer edges of Brixton; but local residents do have their own secret cinema.

It's not easy to find. You have to navigate a tangle of tyre shops as you come out of Loughborough Junction station. Most of the railway arches are occupied by mechanics, but in one a blue neon sign welcomes you

to Whirled Cinema. Press the buzzer and a steep staircase leads straight into the 60-seat screening room. With its sandblasted brick walls, leather benches and cosy lighting, it has the intimacy of a home cinema. There's no box office, just a small bar where you can buy cocktails, coffees, artisan ice cream and posh popcorn.

Before or after the movie, you can sit outside on the terrace or in the bar and get talking movies with fellow members, many of whom are major film buffs. The screenings are a diverse programme of the best of current world and art-house cinema.

Access is for members only – but you can join for just a week, at less than the price of a chain cinema ticket. And the Annual Membership is a steal at £99 – for you plus a guest to see up to 50 films a year. During school term time, there are kids' movies on Saturday mornings, and on the first Thursday of each month they have a documentary night. It's first come, first served, so go early to avoid a last-minute scramble for a seat or you may end up perched at the bar.

After the credits roll, the crowd dissects the film over mojitos and margaritas, their lively chatter interrupted by the occasional train rumbling overhead. Don't worry: they jack up the volume during screenings to drown out the sound effects.

THE PEOPLE'S FRIDGE

Fridge magnates

49 Brixton Station Road, SW9 8PQ
www.peoplesfridge.com
peoplesfridge@gmail.com
07860 021261 (text only)
Monday–Thursday 9am–7pm, Friday–Sunday 9am–5pm
Tube station: Brixton

If you push past all the funky crowds, foodie stalls, pop-up bars and vintage shops crammed under the Pop Brixton roof, right at the back you will find Freddie, the coolest dude in the room. Freddie is The People's Fridge. He's got food for anyone that needs it. And if you've got some you don't need, you can give it to him and he'll keep it safe for someone who does. Local restaurants regularly stock the fridge. There are no restrictions on who can take from it, no stigma involved. The people behind The People's Fridge are … just behind The People's Fridge. The glass doors overlooking Freddie are Impact Hub's offices, a co-working space for freelancers and social entrepreneurs. In 2016 they ran an MIT-designed course called u.lab, which helps create collaborative change in communities. They chose food inequality as their focus: so many people living in food poverty, and

yet so much good food going to waste. How could they join these two up? During an online forum, someone posted about a community fridge in Spain – and the idea seemed to fit perfectly. They set up a crowdfunding campaign to raise the money to buy the fridge, and not only hit their target, but doubled it. So they were able to create a bespoke fridge shelter, and host events to encourage more community sharing.

It wasn't all plain sailing – they had to overcome council concerns about safety and management, and relocate Freddie from the planned front-of-house location to the back of the market. But that turned out to have its advantages because it gives people some privacy. They worked out a staff rota and some food safety rules – no raw meat, raw fish or opened milk, and only food businesses can donate cooked foods. Individuals can give fruit, vegetables, bread and unopened packaged foods. One of the other outreach events that has emerged is Open Project Night: an evening where everyone is welcome to come to Impact Hub Brixton, meet people, eat food and exchange ideas. "We make food central to the evenings", they say, "because it has this amazing ability to create a sense of sharing. It crosses divides and helps people to open up and connect more easily." Open Project Night runs at Impact Hub Brixton every Monday from 6.30pm, and you're welcome to go eat with them, or email to arrange a project tour. Perhaps you might help cook up something even more brilliant than Freddie.

THE CLINK

Pros and cons

Her Majesty's Prison Brixton, Jebb Avenue, SW2 5XF
020 8678 9007
theclinkcharity.org
brixton@theclinkrestaurant.com
Monday—Friday breakfast 8.15am—10am, lunch 12pm—3pm, afternoon tea
2pm—4pm, Thursday gourmet dinner 6pm—9pm
Tube station: Brixton or Stockwell
Buses: 45, 59, 109, 118, 133, 159, 250

I'm going to jail today. It's a short sentence – just two hours of Her Majesty's pleasure, and hopefully mine and the ladies I'm lunching with. We're booked into The Clink, a prison-based restaurant which trains inmates for work in the hospitality industry. The list of things you can't take inside is quite long. There's the obvious tech and weapon stuff, but also no maps, sunglasses or hats (an old-fashioned disguised break-out could still work). No tissues which could be impregnated with drugs. No Blu Tack, gum or anything impressionable (well, apart from us). Me and the other jailbirds put everything except our credit cards in the locker and head towards the high walls.

The first huge Victorian arched doorway squeals and creaks as it slides open. High overhead mirrors provide an overview as a thorough body

search is conducted. Don't arrive too hungry as all this security process can take half an hour. Eventually we are escorted through into the prison yard. Razor wires curl overhead. Six jail wings surround. The old prison governor's house we're heading for has distinctly bar-like wrought iron on the windows.

But once we're inside, it's a contemporary chic dining room with brown slate walls and large purple cakebox lampshades. The menu is modern British, with blurbs for each item which describe not how it tastes, but what it teaches the students: "Learning how to de-bone a chicken is a key skill taught under unit 223." Our waiter is Rosca, a very polite and friendly young man who has gained his City & Guilds NVQ and already has two job offers awaiting his release. He recommends the sea bass starter and it's really good – three little silver-skinned squares of grilled fillet on a courgette ratatouille, drizzled with a lemon reduction and decorated with delicate basil leaf crisps. Someone in the kitchen thoroughly deserves unit 220.

You can come to the Clink for breakfast, lunch, high tea or the Thursday-night gourmet dinner. There's no alcohol on the menu but they mix a mean mocktail. Most of their vegetables are grown in Clink gardens, and the eggs laid by Clink hens, providing not just fresh nutrition but horticulture and animal husbandry training. Graduates are often employed by big-name chains like Wahaca, Carluccio's and Thistle Hotels. Reoffending rates have been reduced by nearly 50%. It's such an excellent project, I might have to go back one morning for some more porridge.

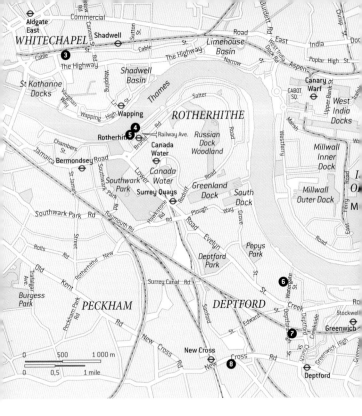

Whitechapel to Woolwich

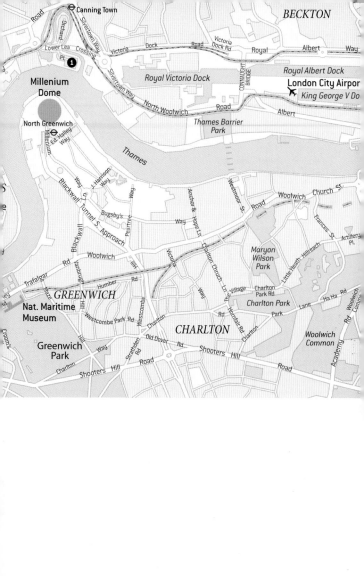

FAT BOY'S DINER

①

Mobile kitsch-in

Trinity Buoy Wharf, 64 Orchard Place, Docklands, E14 0JW
07956 617 902
www.fatboysdiner.co.uk
Monday–Wednesday 8.30am–5pm, Thursday–Saturday 8.30am–9pm,
Sunday 10am–5pm
Tube/DLR station: Canning Town or East India
Bus: D3

Fat Boy's Diner is located at the end of a lobe of Docklands where the river Lea twists down to the Thames, opposite the 02 Arena. Trinity Buoy Wharf was named for the wooden buoys manufactured here from the early 19th century. It's still home to London's only lighthouse, built in 1864 to test maritime lighting equipment and to train lighthouse keepers. The old gas works and boiler rooms have been turned into workshops for carpenters and costumiers, and a community of artists and designers have taken up residence in Container City, colourful stacks of corrugated shipping containers. A photography and recording studio are housed in two lightboats moored nearby.

Parked between a parkour academy and an art school, the red and chrome mobile diner appears to have landed on the quayside from another time and place. It has: Fat Boy's was built in New Jersey in 1941. For 49 years, the diner was parked on the banks of the Susquehana River

in Pennsylvania. After a stint at Spitalfields market, it relocated here in 2001, when there was nothing but tumbleweed.

The bona fide interior, with its chrome bar and leatherette booths, is often used for film and fashion shoots. Thankfully, with new ownership since the last edition, the food has now vastly improved. The burgers are freshly made, the halloumi is griddled just right, and there are healthier options like wraps and salads. On weekdays it's a lovely quiet spot with some seating outside – perfect to watch the sunset.

At weekends you can step inside the lighthouse to listen to "Longplayer," a mesmerising musical composition playing in real time, without repetition, for a thousand years. Next door is London's smallest museum, The Faraday Effect, a tiny hut celebrating the Victorian scientist Michael Faraday, who pioneered the electric generator here.

NEARBY
The Gun ②

27 Coldharbour, Docklands, E14 9NS
0207 519 0075
www.thegundocklands.com

The Gun, a fine bistro pub, which has existed here since the 1700s, is now hidden by Canary Wharf developments. But this is where Lord Nelson used to meet Lady Emma Hamilton for secret trysts. Ask to see the secret stairway they used to disappear up, now leading to a beautiful private dining room.

WILTON'S MUSIC HALL

Sleeping beauty

1 Graces Alley, Wapping, E1 8JB
020 7702 2789
www.wiltons.org.uk
Mahogany Bar: Monday–Friday 5pm–11pm; check the website for
performance times
Tube station: Tower Hill or Aldgate East

Years ago, I went to Wilton's Music Hall for a wedding party. Decadent and dilapidated, layers of paint peeling by candlelight, the building almost stole the show from the bride and groom. Wilton's has a marriage licence now, so you can get hitched on the stage where knickerless girls once danced the can-can and performers ate live rats. This might not sound romantic, but Wilton's is dead sexy.

The oldest surviving Grand Music Hall in the world, this "shrine of gentle music" opened in 1858. John Wilton converted five terraced houses in an alley near Wapping docks into a hidden auditorium for cabaret acts. The grand staircase was lined with hookers – "a better quality than the whores of Haymarket," according to one Victorian visitor. Punters had to buy a refreshment voucher from the box office; the minimum order was two pints of stout and a pie.

Photos by Peter Dazely

These days, patrons tuck into rum cocktails and stone-baked pizzas in the Mahogany Bar. Long since stripped of its mahogany fittings, the bar is a replica built for Guy Ritchie's Sherlock Holmes remake, which was shot here. Even so, the room oozes faded glamour. There are free acoustic gigs in the bar every Monday night. There's also a separate cocktail bar. The main hall hosts a programme of "world-class theatre and exceptional music."

The music hall's heyday didn't last long. With industrialisation, the area soon became more slum than sauce. Wilton's giant chandelier with 27,000 pieces of crystal was sold off to cover running costs. The place closed in 1880. After trying to shut it down for years, the local Methodist mission moved in, staying until 1956. They served 2,000 meals a day during the 1889 dockers' strike, which spawned Britain's first trade union. Wilton's served as a refuge for anti-fascist protestors during the 1936 Battle of Cable Street, and a bomb shelter during the war. It would have been torn down to make way for council flats, if John Betjeman hadn't launched a campaign for the building to be listed.

George Leybourne became an overnight sensation after his song "Champagne Charlie" was first performed at Wilton's. Moët & Chandon bought him a townhouse in Mayfair and paid him to drive through Hyde Park daily, drinking champagne in a carriage drawn by six white horses. He died of liver failure aged 42.

Photo by Peter Dazely

MIDNIGHT APOTHECARY

Campfire cocktails

Brunel Museum roof garden
Railway Avenue, Rotherhithe, SE16 4LF
07917 548475
www.themidnightapothecary.co.uk
lottie@themidnightapothecary.co.uk
Friday and Saturday: evenings in summer, plus occasional autumn dates
Rail/Tube station: Rotherhithe, Bermondsey or Canada Water
Buses: 381, C10

Photo by Sam Spicer

Those with a fear of heights need not worry – the roof of the Brunel Museum is only a few feet above ground level. It is actually the dome over the original shaft entrance to the world's first under-river tunnel, built by Marc Isambard Brunel, with some help from his famous son, Isambard Kingdom.

The space was a bit of a bramble thicket when local gardener Lottie Muir approached the museum's director, Robert Hulse, with the idea of creating a roof garden. Robert, who along with a band of volunteers had transformed the place from a barely open, child-averse trainspotters' club, into a welcoming boutique family museum, loved the plan. Lottie created a ring of raised beds around a circle of benches, and filled them with all kinds of herbs and edible flowers, spiked with towering cardoons and wreathed with hops and vines. It was magical. "What else can we do?" asked Robert one day. And off the top of her head Lottie said, "What about cocktails?" And so the Midnight Apothecary was born.

Visitors sip their drinks under the night sky around a campfire, and toast marshmallows on thick whittled sticks, surrounded by the wafting scents of the garden – chocolatey mints, lemony verbenas, pineappley geraniums. At the side is a little wooden shack where Lottie and her team mix foraged natural ingredients into delicious drinks – my favourite was a raspberry and scented geranium sour mixed with thyme and lemon verbena, available both with and without alcohol. There's also a little food truck on hand for hunger. It's so romantic and enchanting, you'd better be careful not to get carried away – people have proposed and got married here.

It has also attracted an entirely different crowd to the historical romance of engineering. The entrance fee includes a descent to the grand hall below, where actor Tim Thomas (co-composer of the theme tune to kids' TV show *Rainbow*) tells tales of the ingenious innovations involved in the construction of the Thames Tunnel. Rather than dig ineffectively down into the silty mud, the engineers built a vast brick ring which sank down under its own weight. The resulting cathedral-like space opened in 1843 as an underground fairground, visited by Queen Victoria and heralded as the 8th wonder of the world. In the colder months the apothecaries move down here for cabaret and cocktails.

NEARBY

Sands Films Studio ⑤

82 St Marychurch Street, SE16 4HZ
020 7231 2209
www.sandsfilms.co.uk

The building next door is the Sands Films Studio, which has been making independent films since 1975. They have a monthly cinema club which gets booked up fast and also house the Rotherhithe Picture Research Library, an amazing research archive.

More secret gardens

One of London's greatest secret pleasures is to breakfast with the birds, or to have your tea served on a terrace, surrounded by scented blooms. Here's a bouquet of alfresco dining rooms where you can replenish your own cells with air, light and water – and synthesise enough energy to stay rooted in the harsh city conditions.

CHISWICK HOUSE CAFÉ

Chiswick House & Gardens Trust, Burlington Lane, Chiswick, W4 2RP
020 8995 6356 – www.chiswickhouseandgardens.org.uk/visit/cafe-shop
Chiswick House, an 18th-century Palladian villa, provided a bucolic backdrop for some of London's wildest parties. In 1844, the Duke of Devonshire recruited four giraffes to entertain his 700 guests, including Tsar Nicholas I of Russia. The minimalist café next door is a less extravagant affair, but it does great breakfasts and is set in the glorious park where The Beatles shot the video for Paperback Writer.

QUINCE TREE CAFÉ

Clifton Nurseries, 5a Clifton Villas, Little Venice, W9 2PH
020 7432 1867 – www.clifton.co.uk/the-quince-tree-cafe-london
You could easily lose a whole day at this romantic café in London's oldest gardening centre, which has an outside terrace where you can sit in the sunshine, and a cosy greenhouse to shelter in during chillier weather. Their signature brunch is "scrumper" – smashed avocado, hummus, mushrooms, tomatoes on rye with poached eggs and sweet chilli.

KENSINGTON ROOF GARDENS

99 Kensington High Street, Kensington, W8 5SA
At the time of writing, the amazing gardens 100 feet above Kensington High Street are closed. We hope they will soon find new owners for the one-and-a-half acre wonderland of Spanish, Tudor and English woodland gardens which were first opened in 1938, on top of the state-of-the-Art Deco department store. In the meantime we hope someone is feeding the fish and four resident flamingos.

OGNISKO

55 Exhibition Road, South Kensington, SW7 2PG
020 7589 0101 – www.ogniskorestaurant.co.uk
This Polish émigrés' club has been around for over 70 years. Beyond the dining room is a secluded terrace overlooking Prince's Gardens, where you can tuck into smoked salmon blinis, or sweet cheese and orange pancakes, as you work your way through the list of flavoured vodkas.

TANGERINE DREAM CAFÉ

66 Royal Hospital Road, Chelsea, SW3 4HS
020 7349 6464 – www.tangerinedream.uk.com

The sweet and savoury treats are as heavenly as the setting in Chelsea Physic Garden, London's oldest botanical gardens. You'll have to cough up the hefty entrance fee to access the gardens (open April to October), but it's worth it.

BURGH HOUSE BUTTERY

New End Square, Hampstead, NW3 1LT
020 7794 3943 – www.burghhouse.org.uk

Built in 1703, Burgh House is one of the oldest houses in Hampstead. Now home to a small museum commemorating the local community, the basement café is a little-known hideaway. On a sunny afternoon, taking tea and scones in the secret garden is like visiting an old friend's country house. Midweek, you'll only have the birds, the bees, and a few old fogeys for company. At weekends, you'll have to contend with the walkers striding off Hampstead Heath. The staff are friendly and the food is fantastic: feast on carrot, squash and ginger soup served piping hot in its own pot, with a warm buttered cheese and chive scone, macaroni cheese with herbed breadcrumbs, or lamb tagine with coriander couscous, while you fantasise about living in one of the surrounding townhouses.

CANDID CAFÉ

3–5 Torrens Street, Angel, EC1V 1NQ
020 7837 4237 (weekdays)
020 7278 9368 (evenings & weekends)
www.candidarts.com

Candid Arts provides cheap studios and exhibition galleries for recent arts graduates in two crumbling Victorian warehouses on an Islington cul-de-sac. Upstairs is a bohemian café decorated with junk-shop finds, with a long communal table and a wall of windows looking onto a courtyard, a sweet little summer hideaway. Hippy tunes, lentil stew, gentle service.

MUDCHUTE KITCHEN

Mudchute City Farm, Mudchute Park & Farm, Pier Street, Isle of Dogs, E14 3HP
020 3069 9290 – www.mudchute.org

London's largest city farm is in the least likely location – a muddy park overshadowed by the high-rise towers of Canary Wharf. If you like your food fresh-cooked and served with the sounds of the farmyard, you should also try Hackney City Farm and Surrey Docks Farm.

DOG AND BELL

A pretty pickle

116 Prince Street, Deptford, SE8 3JD
020 8692 5664
www.facebook.com/TheDogandBell
thedogandbell@gmail.com
Monday—Sunday 12pm—11pm/12am
Rail station: Deptford
Buses: 47, 199, 188

The Dog and Bell has been standing since at least 1741, and is even mentioned in a 1785 journal by its current name, derived from the bell hung round a dog's neck when duck hunting. The pub was once slap bang in the busy hub of Deptford docks, the Admiralty's point of departure for the entire British Empire. But when the ships all sailed away, the docks gradually reverted to wasteland, leaving the Dog and Bell marooned: there's only one road in.

But make the walk up Watergate Street and you'll be well rewarded. Keep going until you hit a cherry red pub surrounded by a thick moat of beer kegs. Seamus O'Neill took it on in 2016. Drawing on his West Cork family's publican experience, he wanted a place where you can drink real ales, eat great food and get talking proper nonsense with strangers and friends alike. He kept the old billiards table, added a beer garden criss-crossed by strings of glowing globe bulbs, and went with the Deptford predilection for a festival.

It must be said, Seamus loves a festival. He puts on a proper show for all the Celtic fests – St Patrick, St Andrews, Burns Night. Then there's also Mayday, Halloween, the Real Ale Festival, the Cider and Perry Festival … There's hardly a week goes past when they're not celebrating something. Each time, his artist (and wife) in residence creates amazing window displays, while Seamus heads off to tiny far-flung breweries and brings back rare small-batch ales.

Possibly the most important date is November's annual Pickle Festival. A sort of pub-based village fete, there are competitive categories for all kinds of preserves, cakes, even ceramics. The judges are the public, who queue up to taste, scribbling their scores on paper plates. It's not the most scientific system – the entrants themselves are allowed to vote, and some pickles get tasted more than others. "The secret to winning …" says Seamus, leaning in and lowering his voice, " … is a large jar."

People are still put out by 2017's pickle winner, who had no previous preserving experience and won with a brightly coloured recipe she'd downloaded from the internet. "It's not about me," said one contender whose traditional brown medlar jelly had lost out to the gaudy upstart, "it's about the wider pickle community." But don't let the drama of the Picksticle make you wait for November: this is the perfect place to get pickled any month of the year.

BUSTER MANTIS

(7)

Arch revolution

3–4 Resolution Way, Deptford, SE8 4NT
020 8691 5191
www.bustermantis.com
hello@bustermantis.com
Tuesday–Thursday 6pm–11.30pm, Friday 6pm–1.30am, Saturday 5pm –1.30am,
Sunday 2pm–11.30pm
Rail/Tube station: Deptford or New Cross

Emerging from Deptford's recently renovated train station, you are faced with a wave of funky eateries in the vaults supporting London's oldest passenger railway. It looks like a happening, thriving place. But the first bar to open up, before Deptford had its makeover, is hidden on the other side of the tracks. The third and fourth arches down on Resolution Way are home to Buster Mantis, a great Jamaican bar, restaurant and music club which was set up in 2016 by local resident Gordon McGowan.

There's something of a family tradition of being the first to take the plunge. Gordon's grandfather was one of the original Windrush arrivals – you can see him in full RAF uniform on the Pathé footage of the ship docking in 1948. His parents kept up the entrepreneurial spirit, setting up a little café called Irie in nearby New Cross. An art

school graduate, Gordon had long hoped someone else would open the kind of bar where he and his mates would like to go eat, drink and listen to music. Eventually he got tired of waiting and decided he would have to do it himself. At least my mates will come, he thought.

Gordon designed Buster Mantis with gentle nods to his island heritage. The name is a phonetic play on Jamaica's first prime minister, Sir Alexander Bustamante. Avoiding the Rasta beach shack cliché, the place is quietly sophisticated: a pineapple outline logo, a delicious rum punch and cocktail list, all served with a relaxed, laid-back vibe which seems to emanate from Gordon himself. The menu is contemporary Jamaican, overseen by Gordon's mum, Janet, a great cook, who pops by daily to check things are good.

And they're really, really good: the saltfish fritters with tamarind and pineapple relish are the perfect balance of light, crispy and chewy. I ask my friends to describe the jerk chicken wings we are eating, and in between mouthfuls they blurt out "sticky," "spicy," "sucky," "sexy" (at which point I realise the rum punch is quite strong).

The other B.M. vault is a changing event venue and creative space – exhibitions, life-drawing classes, film festivities. Wednesday nights are "Steamdown" – a live band night where people don't just sit and clap appreciatively from behind their cocktails. By the look of the crowd dancing crazily to the afro jazz sounds, these arches are a definite hit with more than just Gordon's mates.

OUT OF THE BREW

A breath of fresh air

306 New Cross Road, New Cross, SE14 6AF
020 8265 6740
www.outofthebrewcafe.com
mel@outofthebrewcafe.com
Monday–Saturday 8.30am–6.30pm
Tube/Rail station: New Cross Gate or New Cross

Out of the Brew café's sky-blue shop front overlooks the corner of New Cross where the highway grime of the A20 and the A2 meet. Heavy traffic trundles past – cross-Channel lorries and stressed-out southbound drivers, all in too much of a rush to stop except to thump their steering wheel at being stuck in a traffic jam.

But step into Out of the Brew and all that pressure seems to slip away. The light floods in through the big glass window and pours off the yellow and white walls. The counter displays healthy light food – soups, sandwiches and salads – balanced by the temptation of delicious-looking cakes. Big Kilner jars of jams and chutneys sit proudly, homemade from locally grown ingredients. Very local indeed: head through the back door and you'll find the rhubarb patch. And there you'll also unearth a little orchard with apples, pears, Morello cherries, golden raspberries and even a peach tree. The walls are covered by vines and figs, and in the gaps are flora & fauna themed mosaics made by local school kids. It's like you've accidentally stepped into provincial France.

There's a little grassy lawn, with picnic tables against the wall and a cluster of blue-painted cable reels at the side. On sunny evenings they have a secret outdoor cinema, with movies accompanied by popcorn and summer cocktails – cucumber gimlets and elderflower margaritas, priced around a pretty reasonable £6 mark. If it's raining they screen the films inside, the main window transforming into the big screen.

There may also be bands playing, artists exhibiting, poets reading, comedians, er … standing up. Goldsmiths is just nearby so there's a steady supply of art school creatives. Sometimes the events are down in "Under the Brew" – the bright whitewashed basement room, which makes for fun acoustics. But the best thing is just eating your salad al fresco on a sunny afternoon, with the scent of the fig leaves wafting around as you think: why drive all the way down to Dover when you can cross to the Continent right here?

FAN MUSEUM ORANGERY

A fan-tastic tea room

12 Crooms Hill, Greenwich, SE10 8ER
020 8305 1441
www.thefanmuseum.org.uk
info@thefanmuseum.org.uk
Tuesday, Friday, Saturday and Sunday 12.30pm–4pm (only to museum visitors)
DLR/Rail station: Cutty Sark or Greenwich

One of the smallest, strangest museums in London, The Fan Museum opened in 1991 but feels as though it's been here for centuries. Housed in two Georgian townhouses in Greenwich, the museum contains founder Hélène Alexander's exquisite collection of over 4,000 fans and related objects (even the soap in the bathroom is fan-shaped). Most of the fans are stored in cedar-lined drawers to prevent damage and decay. The function of those on display varies wildly: fashion accessories, status symbols, ceremonial tools, political flags or advertising giveaways. At the apogee of their popularity at the turn of the 19th century, a whole "fan language" developed. A fan resting upon the lips meant "I don't trust you;" hiding the sunlight implied "You are ugly."

If the museum is a whimsical time warp, so is The Orangery tucked away in the garden. The whole room is decorated with a hand-painted mural of a pastoral scene, featuring a three-dimensional fan, *trompe l'œil* insects and flowerpots, as well as various Greenwich landmarks. Tables are daintily set beneath shimmering blue Murano chandeliers. Naturally, the napkins are decorated with fan prints. Peter Whittaker, the spry old house manager who lives on site, brings warm scones with clotted cream and plum jam made by Mrs Alexander. Full tea also includes simple sponge cakes or Bakewell tart made locally (but no sandwiches). In this enchanting glasshouse, you can't fail to slow down and feel that all's well with the world.

Sadly, the delightful Japanese gardens, with their fan-shaped flowerbeds, aren't open to the public thanks to the disobliging neighbours. This seems particularly churlish given that the museum only receives about 8,000 visitors a year, mostly grannies and fashion students. Even so, with only half a dozen tables, it can fill up quickly and there's no reservations. If you have to queue, try rapidly opening and closing your fan – that'll hurry them up.

NEARBY

Oliver's Jazz Bar ⑩

9 Nevada Street, Greenwich, SE10 9JL
020 8858 3693
www.oliversjazzbar.com

Intimate and shambolic, this is a late-night jazz bar in the old mould. Hidden down a gated alley, the black and red basement bar could be in Montmartre. Seasoned pros and precocious students from Trinity College of Music jam on the threadbare stage every night. The goateed Gallic owner, Olivier, serves "only liquid food, no fancy cocktails."

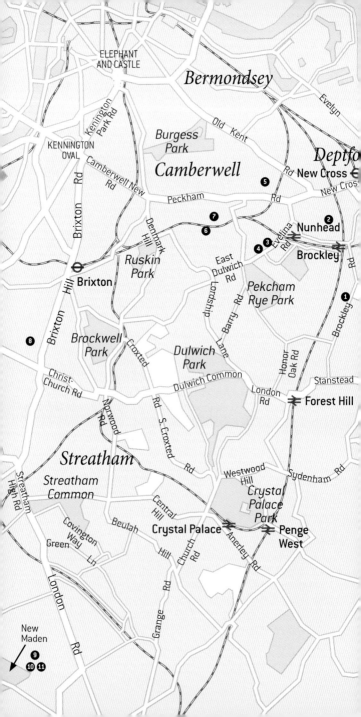

Greater London South East

RIVOLI BALLROOM

Sex in the suburbs

346–350 Brockley Road, Crofton Park, SE4 2BY
020 8692 5130
www.rivoliballroom.com
rivoliballroom@live.com
Open first Saturday and first and third Sunday of the month; check website for other one-off events
Rail station: Crofton Park or Brockley then 15-minute walk
Buses: 171, 172, 122

It requires effort to reach the Rivoli Ballroom, but the schlep to deepest suburbia is worth it: this is surely one of London's sexiest venues. Despite its art deco frontage, you might walk right past the Rivoli, if it weren't for the vintage car parked outside. On either side of the entrance, two original signs read "Dancing" and "Tonight". People still come here to dance, but sadly it's no longer open every night.

The Rivoli opened as Crofton Park Picture Palace in 1913. Like many cinemas, it closed in the 1950s as television gripped the nation. After a makeover by local dance enthusiast Leonard Tomlin, it reopened as the Rivoli Ballroom in 1959. Tomlin's flamboyant interior – a riot of neoclassical, art deco and oriental motifs – is intact. A foyer with marquetry panelling leads to the ballroom, a vaulted vision of scarlet and gold. The walls are lined with red velour and gilt encrusted with diamanté.

Photo: Rivoli Ballroom © Peter Dazeley from his book *London Uncovered*

Couples glide across the sprung maple dance floor, their sparkly frocks shimmering beneath crystal chandeliers, Chinese lanterns and disco balls.

Two bars flank the ballroom: one with red leather booths and an Arabesque tiled bar, the other with gold flock wallpaper and a mosaic ceiling. Even the etiquette is old fashioned: the barmaid calls you "Miss" and everyone waits in a single line to order drinks.

The first Sunday of the month is devoted to ballroom dancing, with owner Bill Mannix acting as DJ. Now in his 70s, Bill has run the Rivoli for over 30 years but none of the regulars have ever seen him dance. Everyone else does, though. Glamorous couples of all ages foxtrot and quickstep across the room like Fred Astaire and Ginger Rogers. Many of the dancers have worked as extras on films shot at the Rivoli. It's occasionally used for concerts and music videos; Tina Turner and Florence and the Machine have both taken to the stage.

Regular events include the popular Rouges 70s/80s disco night, pop-up cinema screenings, and the monthly Jive Party, with live bands playing vintage Americana. The evening starts with a jive dance class for beginners and ends with a rockabilly crowd sweating it out to lindy hop. At Jacky's Jukebox on the first Saturday of the month, men go into the ladies boudoir and come out dressed as women and the music segues from Louis Prima to *Saturday Night Fever*. Then there's The Magic Theatre, where guests must "dress to impress, astonish and entice" – just like the Rivoli Ballroom itself.

London's secret salsa scene

There's a whole underworld of salsa going on across London. A network of halls and back rooms where addicts meet two or three times a week. You can't tell who's got a serious habit by just looking at them: they can be any age, come from any country – they could be lawyers, chefs, IT techs, psychologists, plumbers, historians. They speak in a special code – On1, On2, cross body, Cuban, hammerlock, copa, shines. When they dance together they look like they've been rehearsing for months, and yet they might be total strangers …

If you've ever fancied trying your hand at salsa dancing and you thought you'd start with a Saturday night trip to Bar Salsa! in Charing Cross, you may have been put off for life. There are some great teachers and DJs there, but on the wrong night, the dance floor can be invaded by spectators who can't dance, or have had too much to drink, or are just there to pick up girls (or usually all three). Most salsa dancers don't drink, not while they're out dancing anyway – there's far too much concentration and co-ordination required. So lots of the venues don't really have bars – or if they do, the bar tenders look pretty pissed off because all anyone ever asks them for is tap water. They resign themselves to lining up water jugs with a pile of cups and leave people to it.

In London's beginner-friendly, high-quality salsa scene, you'll find classes to suit your level at a venue near you. You don't need to have a partner to go to any of these places; you rotate dance partners in class, and you'll quickly get to know people. One of the best central venues to start with is **Incognito Dance** (www.incognitodance.com) on Wednesday nights by Hammersmith Bridge. It's a beautiful old dance hall where they teach drop-in classes of all levels running simultaneously, with a bonus sensual *bachata* class before hand, and a late-running social (dance party) afterwards, which is not too intimidating for beginners. The same team run nights at five other venues where you can use their vouchers.

On Sunday evenings, in the heart of the Royal National Hotel – a '70s Soviet-style behemoth in Bloomsbury – you'll find the longest-running salsa night in Europe: **SOS** (Salsa on Sundays). They have been lovingly laying out their black-and-white dance floor since January 2000. Their friendly evenings start with four levels of classes – how to be invited into the top level is perhaps the biggest secret in salsa …

It's worth travelling further west to Northfields, where you'll find an excellent, more personal place to learn at **Pexava** (www.pexava.com), who hold classes with a mini-social in the Navasartian Centre on Tuesday nights. Their smaller venue means you can really see and hear the instructors, who are passionate about teaching good technique (the secret to how those strangers dance so well together). They've just started in Islington on Thursday nights too.

Twice a month they hold full social dances in the beautiful Conway Hall near Holborn, where the city's serious salseros gather for a hard-core salsa fix.

Up north, at the Boston Music Room in Tufnell Park, you'll find **Funky Mambo** (www.funkymambo.com), formerly known as TNT – the inner On2 cult of the London salsa scene, where the most addicted dancers go when they can't get enough of a fix from the prevalent "ONE two three" step, and need a harder, New York style "One TWO three" hit. It's a subtle difference but it's properly narcotic. A very similar crowd go to the nearby **Cha Cha Social** (chachasocial.london) with a 50:50 mix of mambo and cha cha, the slightly slower and even more intoxicating On2 dance.

Head south to Balham and Stockwell and you'll discover **Miguel Mayana** (www.miguelmayana.co.uk) cooking up a special mix – of classes On1, On2, with a splash of contemporary and Afro-Cuban. Their hugely fun monthly socials are called *Que Rico!* and used to be the hottest in London but they've thankfully sorted the air conditioning. If you venture into the back, you'll find a secret dark room dedicated to the intimate art of kizomba.

In Paddington you'll find **Caramelo** (www.caramelolatindance.co.uk), a school teaching every type of Latin dance in a formal monthly course structure. The more four-week classes you sign up for, the cheaper it gets, but be careful – aim too high on the bargain scale and at the end of the month you may be unable to walk …

There are loads of other places running fortnightly or monthly socials which all kick off with classes. **Hot Salsa** mix LA and Cuban style at the Aeronaut in Acton, and **I Like it Like That** throw salsa socials in Holborn and at Pop Brixton, with great DJs playing vinyl. Once a year **FK Dance** (www.fkdance.com) runs **ABCD** – Any Body Can Dance – an intense day of workshops and classes in Chalk Farm, ending in a massive dance party.

Mambo City (www.mambocity.co.uk) hold classes and events all over town, and indeed the world, but a central favourite is their monthly salsa and kizomba social at ULU Student Central. They also organise the huge annual Salsa Congresses, where dancers, teachers and performers convene from all over the world and see nothing of London except for the dance floor of a Heathrow hotel.

When you first venture out from a class and into a social, it can seem intimidating. Dancers may appear snobby to beginners, but just think of it like tennis – it can get a little boring for an advanced player when their opposite constantly misses the ball. But they were all beginners once, so if they're good people they will give you a dance: just be brave and ask. And remember: in salsa, the ladies are encouraged to ask the gents to dance, so don't stand waiting – get on that floor and get high!

CHAI'S GARDEN

An unlikely partnership

1 Kitto Road, Nunhead, SE14 5TW
020 7207 7134
www.skehans.com
Monday—Friday 6pm—11pm, Saturday 5pm—11pm, Sunday 4pm—10pm
Rail station: Nunhead, New Cross or New Cross Gate
Bus: 343

There is a sign for Chai's Garden on the brick wall at the top of Gellatly Road, but it's small, high up and buried by the ivy, on a residential street that only locals are likely to pass. Those who stumble across it do so through the back of Skehans Irish pub, which towers above with its Guinness, live music nights and outdoor multi-level beer deck. While down below is a tranquil little glasshouse serving ornate Thai dishes surrounded by *Sala* huts and flowers, with a little wooden spirit house in the corner watching over it all. And maybe thinking: British pubs and Thai food, what an unlikely pairing.

If it's just because spicy food goes well with beer, then why isn't an Indian arrangement more commonplace? Have pub landlords married Thai girls in their droves and then set them up in their kitchens? In fact, the answer seems to originate with the entrepreneurial and hard-working Thais, who have experienced British drinking culture in Bangkok and figured wisely that pubs are a good location for a food business. One of the first places to do it was the beautiful Churchill Arms in Notting Hill, where in 1990 a Thai chef approached landlord Gerry O'Brien with what was then a totally bizarre idea. But the Irishman took a chance and Londoners loved the surprise combination.

Chai came to Britain as a teenager to stay with her aunt, who ran the Pat Pong restaurant in Chingford. She wanted to branch out on her own so she approached Bill Skehan, who was managing a pub in Islington, suggesting she run the food there. Elegant, effervescent Chai and solid Irish joker Bill got on as well as *pad Thai* and a pint. Having experienced the Islington effect in Upper Street, they figured the same could happen in Nunhead ...

So they took the plunge and decamped to the huge old Irish neighbourhood pub with only a handful of regulars. It took some serious love and hard work to get the pub back on its feet – and after ten years, the promised Upper Street effect is only just getting started. Bill has now retired and his nephew Brian has taken over. And a younger more diverse crowd is coming, spilling out back and spotting the carved wooden huts below. They find good-value Thai classics with pub-priced drinks in a beautiful setting – perfect to share with a *Sala* load of friends. And if you don't meet Chai there, you'll find her in her Croydon hair salon – she's unstoppable.

THE BEER SHOP LONDON

The art of ale

40 Nunhead Green, Nunhead, SE15 3QF
020 7732 5555
www.thebeershoplondon.co.uk
hello@thebeershoplondon.co.uk
Tuesday —Friday 4pm—11/11.30pm, Saturday 12pm—11.30pm, Sunday 12pm —8pm
Rail station: Nunhead, Peckham Rye or Queens Road Peckham
Buses: 78, P12

The Beer Shop London is a shop by name and a shop by appearance, but step inside and you'll find a kind of cross between a pub, deli, living room and art gallery. It was set up by a local husband and wife team: beardy, beer-obsessed barman Lee, and neither beardy nor beer-obsessed art programmer Lauren. They decided to combine their work and start the kind of place that they would want to go for a friendly drink, and that would include a creative space for artists.

Inspired by the micropubs down in Broadstairs where Lee's mum lives, they converted a vacant shop on the edge of Nunhead Green into a bar – installing taps for locally brewed beers (some really great microbreweries have sprung up in the area) and a fridge for an extraordinary selection of bottled and canned independent British brews. Drink on the premises or takeaway – they'll even bottle the fresh stuff for you. Come on the right day and you can meet the brewers themselves.

And for the artists? A blank wall, where commissioned painters, illustrators and designers can create something amazing. A bit like Tate Modern's Turbine Hall, but much much smaller (and in a shop selling beer). The pieces change every six months and have included Matthew Kay's humorous "Diagram Poems," Jemma Egan's giant "Dot to Dot" picture and Miriam Nice's hoppy mural of beer-making plants.

But don't let the art make you think the place is stuffy or precious. This is a proper locals' hang-out, with an informal, welcoming atmosphere. On summer Fridays and Saturdays, the back garden becomes home to a changing street food pop up – you might find Japanese Okonomiyaki, Basque-style tapas or Eastern European grills. Lauren or Lee will be on hand at the bar to advise which is the best drink to accompany the food.

Or the other way round: on Takeaway Tuesdays, you can bring your own dinner to complement your drinks. Just next door is the fantastic fishmongers, Sopers, who will shuck you a Galway Bay oyster for 95 pence – a dozen for £10.95. A few pence extra and they'll throw in a platter with ice and seaweed – or you can bring your own vessel. Grab a lemon from the grocers and stuff a bottle of Tabasco in your pocket and you've got yourself a very fine BYO dinner indeed.

BABETTE

French evolution

57 Nunhead Lane, Nunhead, SE15 3TR
020 3172 2450
www.facebook.com/babettenunhead
babettenunhead@gmail.com
Wednesday and Thursday 4pm–11pm, Friday and Saturday 10am–12am,
Sunday 11pm–7pm
Rail station: Nunhead
Buses: 78, P12

A few bends up the road from Nunhead's village green, Babette looks from the outside like it's still an old pub – ghostly traces of the Truman lettering still visible through the white paint. Only the letter B hanging above clues you in. So you may be surprised when you swing the "Public Bar" doors open and find not a beery old local but a bright, spacious café/restaurant with smiling staff, well-chosen lampshades and shelves lined with dark green Apilco coffee cups.

Babette was living in Paris when an old lover turned friend called

to say he'd bought a building in Nunhead. Babette had already transformed a grungy £5,000 attic in the 11th arrondissement into a perfectly appointed loft apartment – could she do something here too? She found a huge, filthy space filled with pigeon droppings and far away from a reasonable footfall. But, she thought, maybe this could be a restaurant ... With her boyish haircut and girlish smile, Babette is imbued with the countercultural socialist spirit of '68. She didn't approach the venture as a business, more as an exciting new life experience. "Work is not the purpose of our lives, work is a platform to transform ourselves," she says in her still heavy French accent. She has a flair for the French *art de la chine* – scouring second-hand shops and *vide-greniers* for a few choice vintage objects, bringing a warm bohemian bourgeois feel to the space (if you wish to *chiner* round the corner, you will find a wall display of bric-a-brac for sale).

Babette's recruitment process was unconventional: "The first person who walks through the door: that will be the person I will work with." And so the staff, from the plasterers to the head chef, came here by accident. After work, they would sit up late, drinking wine, talking about their lives and becoming friends. She encouraged her first chef Sam to be as inventive as he wanted, and so the wonderful Babette sharing platters emerged.

On my visit we feasted on a wooden board crammed with crisp filo cigars of soft smoked haddock, a creamy burrata with caponata and almonds, thick-sliced cured salmon blinis, a scarlet mound of giant couscous with beetroot, and a green pea, pistachio and ricotta puree. The platters are a bit like the space – every piece perfectly chosen and executed, but presented without fuss or ceremony. "If others are happy, we will be happy," proclaims Babette. And sitting in the midst of her warm, thriving space, I think she has her philosophy just right.

ASIDE

A sideline in design

56 Goldsmith Road, Peckham, SE15 5TF
020 7358 1760
asidelondon.com
bookings@asidelondon.com
Wednesday–Friday 6pm–10pm, Saturday 10am–10pm, Sunday 12pm–6pm
Rail station: Queens Road Peckham or Peckham Rye

Aside is definitely off the side of the main action of Peckham – it's in an old terraced house at the end of a quiet residential back street on the north side of Queens Road. When Rob Dunne took it on, he was thinking of it as a repeat of their Old Spike coffee roastery. But then he saw the beautiful parquet floors and the designer in him couldn't bear to destroy the place with big dirty roasting machines. Instead he started to figure out how to turn it into a restaurant.Inside, the design is heavily influenced by the minimalist geometric artist Donald Judd, with whom Rob is so obsessed that he has a Judd-inspired tattoo on his arm. The three simple lines in a disconnected H-shape represent the three steps: awareness, acknowledgement, enlightenment. Judd saw this art philosophy in everything, even the humble table. So the tables in Aside

are simple and yet clever: delicate, modular and with a double deck – a little clutter-reducing shelf just below the top where the cutlery, napkins or your paperback can be stored away. The bench seating around the clean white zigzag double room ensures a relaxed communal feel – more café culture than fine dining. Rob would call it eating: "Most people are more comfortable eating over dining. Something about dining often makes people uncomfortable in themselves."

But the flip side is that the eating here is very fine indeed. Head chef Christian Taylor creates beautiful small plates of locally sourced seasonal produce, with intriguing touches – the beef tartare comes dressed with a charcoal and chilli infused oil, giving it a smoky Turkish *mangal* flavour. A red mullet ceviche is served with elderflower and slithers of green peaches, which have an unusual tart almondy flavour. On Saturdays the menu turns to brunch, and in the early summer poached eggs are served with asparagus and morel mushrooms. Sundays they serve up fantastic roasts with Yorkshire puds and triple-cooked roast potatoes. And there are always delicious desserts, inspired by Christian's nan, who was something of a pudding guru.

Outside, there are blue benches against the white walls, where in the summer you can sip a glass of chilled rose and share terrace menu finger foods. If you've got an east-facing seat, you can see the brightly coloured faces of the Thierry Noir mural at the far end of the road. And the upside is that it's all out of earshot of Peckham's crazy high street.

GOSNELLS OF LONDON

Honey, trapped

Unit 2, Print Village, Chadwick Road, Peckham, SE15 4PU
020 3289 9562
www.gosnells.co.uk
contact@gosnells.co.uk
Friday 4pm–10pm, Saturday 12pm–10pm
Rail station: Peckham Rye

I f you think of mead as an ancient potion brewed by barefoot monks and supped by warriors from bronze chalices, then an industrial estate in the back roads of Peckham doesn't seem the most likely location for a meadery. But that is where Tom Gosnell practises the ancient art of turning honey into wine. The drink he creates is nothing like the rough stuff from island abbeys. This is modern mead – a light sparkling citrusy number, to be drunk chilled, and more akin to Prosecco than anything else. This is no industrially processed alcohol with super-sweet bee juice bunged in; the honey is there from the start, so most of the sweetness is fermented out. At only 5.5%, it's far more "sessionable" – perfect for a sunny afternoon. In an industrial estate. On the wrong side of the Peckham rail tracks.

London's only meadery – aka the "honey cupboard" – opens as a tap room on Friday and Saturday afternoons with the mead flowing late into the evening. You'll usually find Tom there, busy as a bee, pouring mead direct from a row of beer taps. He also serves several different experimental flavours, which he makes in smaller barrels: hopped mead, hibiscus mead, salted liquorice mead ... In the winter you can sit by the bar on the cluster of plywood stools surrounded by vats of honey and packing crates. Or in the summer there are benches outside, with big pots of leafy green bamboo to take the edge off the metal and tarmac surroundings.

Tom has a hive brain of honey-based knowledge. How the bee starts to turn the gathered nectar into honey even while in transit in his honey stomach: as soon as the nectar passes the bee's tiny brain, it triggers the production of an enzyme called invertase, which starts to break down the honey into its constituent sugars. Once this mix is dropped off at the hive, the other bees fan the sugary liquid to dehydrate it before encasing it in wax storage cells. Otherwise it would ferment on the spot, and then you'd have a bunch of not so busy bees. The honey produced by the

British bee comes from a huge variety of flowers, so Tom uses Spanish honey for a more uniform flavour. But he is currently working on smaller batches of locally produced honey for a truer London terroir. Head down to the honey cupboard to taste the latest in bee-to-bottled brewings.

PECKHAM LIBERAL CLUB

Still swinging

24 Elm Grove, Peckham, SE15 5DE
020 7639 1093
www.peckhamliberalclub.org
peckhamliberalclub@gmail.com
Membership: £20
Monday 11am—5pm, Tuesday and Wednesday 11am—4pm and 6.30pm—11pm,
Thursday—Sunday 11am—11pm
Rail station: Peckham Rye

From the outside, the PLC looks like an old white house at the edge of a residential back street. You might not go in because you mistake it for a branch of the political party. But wander through the warren of wood-veneered corridors, punctuated by squares of electric light from overhead Perspex boxes and it's more like you've entered some kind of East Berlin Communist HQ.

Pass a red phone box in the corner and you remember you're in London. Turn into the main stage room and you'll realise it's the swinging sixties. The stage is framed in gold, backed by glittering curtains and frilled with a matching valance. The herringbone parquet floor below and the geometrical ceiling tiles above convey a certain pride in appearance. Even empty, the room instantly conjures up women with beehives and

Photos by Hanson Leatherby

false eyelashes, and men in suits with narrow ties and pocket squares.

This is not the only perfectly preserved room. There's the lounge with dark velvet low-leaning armchairs and matching studded sofas, the floor diagonals echoed on the patterned mirrors. And there's a vast snooker hall, each table glowing with its own fringed lighting canopy.

It sounds like the place is a film set – and indeed many a movie and pop video have been shot here. But it's actually still a working members' club, and no longer just for men – though, shockingly, women weren't allowed to join until 2006. Now they've got the gender split sorted, the gap they're trying to bridge is a generational one. Most of the younger members are in their sixties, and all round the bar are photos of ones who have passed on. They need young people to join. It only costs £20 for the year, and then you get cheap drinks and the run of one of the most cinematic locations in all of London. There's a great bar where everyone will chat to you, a garden out the back where they sometimes have barbecues, and the diary is packed with concerts and social events.

"You always feel welcome here," says one of the regulars, and it's true. When I visited they were a hoot, telling me about all the celebrities they've had in filming – the likes of Paloma Faith ("a lovely gal"), Dizzee Rascal ("ooh, very violent video"), Barbara Windsor (of course), the "very handsome" Idris Elba, and "that Cumberbatch lad." So get down there and ask a couple of the regulars to second your membership. If you put your hair up and ladle on the mascara, you might even end up in a movie.

HAN BAR AND RESTAURANT

Korea advice

Apex House, 1 High Street, New Malden, KT3 4DQ
020 8949 7730
hanukhan.com
Monday–Thursday 12pm–3pm, 5pm–12.30am, Friday 12pm–3pm, 5pm–
1.30am, Saturday 12pm–4pm, 5pm–1.30am, Sunday 12pm–4pm, 5pm–
12.30am
Rail station: New Malden

I have good friends who live in New Malden and we've eaten at nearly all the high street Korean restaurants, but had never spotted Han. The restaurant's doorway should be the first thing you see when you emerge from the train station, but the dark wood exterior recedes into the shadows of the seventies concrete office tower block above, and the spindly tree attempting to offset the greyness manages to branch over the sign. All you notice is the glare of next-door's express supermarket and the long winding wheelchair ramp. But if you persist, you'll find a restaurant unlike any of its more visible competitors in suburban London's Little Korea.

Here you are transported into rural Korea with raised dining tables set inside four little wooden pavilions or *jeong ja,* their low sweeping roof timbers gracefully skirting the central aisle. If you want a more hip urban feel, further back there's a bar and a side door onto a tiny garden below the railway line where the trendy long-fringed barman and his mates sit drinking like they're in city centre Seoul, not somewhere near Surbiton.

The food, though a little slow in coming, was a hit with our table, which included my friend's two energetic boys. They wolfed down the *goon mandoo* fried dumplings, belted through the beef on rice *bibimbap* and basically inhaled the fresh and extra-crispy Korean fried chicken. They even enjoyed the sliced boneless pork trotters though they couldn't be entirely persuaded to come to terms with the sea whelk salad, which admittedly the adults found a bit on the chewy side. We all loved the accompanying fermented pickled veg – napa cabbage, radish, spinach, beansprouts and turnip. Koreans can pickle anything to crunchy kimchi perfection.

After dinner I took the boys to explore the third setting – the basement karaoke suites. That was a mistake. The room was small, the volume was stuck on DEAFENING and my pre-teen duo had a microphone each. Queue brain seizure as they practise boomboxing in my ears while I frantically scan the huge binder for a code to a familiar song. When I finally manage to navigate the Korean input controls and get anything – ANYTHING – playing, it turns out to be La Macarena and we descend into a seventh hell. Thankfully we are just being treated to a sample song rather than paying for a full hour. I definitely need to lie down in a *jeong ja.*

WOODIES FREEHOUSE

Collage sports

The Sportsground, Thetford Road, New Malden, KT3 5DX
0208 949 5824
www.woodiesfreehouse.co.uk
info@woodiesfreehouse.co.uk
Monday–Thursday 11am–11pm, Friday and Saturday 11am–11.30pm,
Sunday 12pm–11pm
Rail station: New Malden
Buses: 265, K5, K1, 213, 131

Woodies is referred to as New Malden's best-kept secret, and no wonder – it's as if they've put in a major defence to stop you finding it. The A3 dual carriageway cuts off one side, rows of white-harled terraced houses keep guard on the other, and if you approach from the open side, there's a good mile of playing fields to cross before you reach it. Even when you push past the white picket fences and the picnic tables, there's still a last line of covered terrace to tackle. When you finally burst through into the main bar room, you'll discover what they're so keen to guard.

Every inch of this large bar room is plastered with a huge sports-themed collage – team portraits, match tickets, celebrity photos and newspaper cuttings. Programmes for a thousand matches are pinned like bunting to the ceiling beams – mainly football, mainly Wimbledon and Crystal Palace, but plenty of others as well.

In the centre of two walls are rare 1960s photographic murals of historic cricket matches at the Oval. Another depicts an 1849 match between Sussex and Kent at Brighton, the players and crowd dressed in top hats, waistcoats and spats. Nearby there's a golfing cabinet filled with tees, balls and putting heads. The corner to the left of the bar (affectionately nicknamed "death row" on account of the advanced age of the regulars who sit there) displays a packed photo patchwork of local fishermen and their proud catches. This giant sports scrapbook was begun over 25 years ago by Bernard Coleman, who first turned this sports pavilion into a pub. The collection has been replenished over the years with donations by regulars and friends. A major supply came from Ron Noades, former chairman manager of Wimbledon and Crystal Palace football clubs. The ceiling is in a constant state of renewal, as paper programmes disintegrate and get replaced, though there's much on the walls that remains from the original collection.

There are a few non-sports stars – the Queen Mum takes pride of place opposite the bar, and near the kitchen there's a photograph of John Wayne playing darts when he visited. There's plenty of beer memorabilia too – they love their real ales here, and regularly win CAMRA awards. There's also great traditional pub food and plenty of beer and music events to keep you entertained. But remember to travel light – you won't need to bring anything to read.

SING SING

K-Poptastic

11 Coombe Road, New Malden, KT3 4PX
020 8605 0506
www.facebook.com/SingSingYoungStar
singsingbar3@gmail.com
Monday–Sunday 6pm–12am/12.30am
Rail station: New Malden

Sing Sing looks a bit dodgy from the outside: a little red sign above a seedy-looking New Malden doorway. Wander down the narrow corridor, worrying you might be heading into a brothel, and you'll find a front room with saggy sofas and a basic serving hatch bar. But go up the steps and you're suddenly in a vast hall which has all the innocence of a youth club. There are guys playing pool, a giant projector screen TV, and everywhere tables full of kids sharing bowls of Korean bar food and bottles of *Soju* (Korean sake) toasting each shot with cries of "Jjan!"

Round the edges are doors into private rooms which occasionally open to release a sudden blast of totally mental karaoke singing. But I'll quickly close that door for a moment – phew, that's better – and reopen it in a minute when we're all a bit more prepared.

Despite its name, singing isn't the main reason people come to Sing Sing. It's just a great place to hang out with friends. You don't have to be Korean – they will welcome you with big smiles and friendly chat whoever you are. Joo Min and his brother Joo Young took it over from their dad and have made it a lively, happening place. Perfect for tasting fire chicken, steamed omelette or spicy rice cake. Brilliant for watching sports matches on their really well set-up projector screen (especially if it's South Korea v. Japan).

Okay, now back to the singing. I've seen plenty of karaoke over the years and thought I'd gotten the gist of it – one or two people get up and attempt to impress their audience with a wobbly Whitney or a substandard Sinatra. I usually avoid it, ever since I was arm wrestled onto a stage by a couple of girlfriends and discovered that Blondie's "Heart of Glass" was a bad choice without the aid of helium. But Korea-style karaoke – called *noraebang* – is a group activity, and those groups are *very* enthusiastic. I walked through one of the side doors and found myself in a gang of 15 Korean lads, all so intent on jumping around the room and belting their lungs out to K-pop, they didn't even notice me.

If you want to try Sing Sing – or eat eat, drink drink or play play – you should get there fast because the block is under threat of redevelopment. But they'll definitely reopen somewhere nearby, so check their facebook page for wherever they pop pop up next.

Greater London North & West

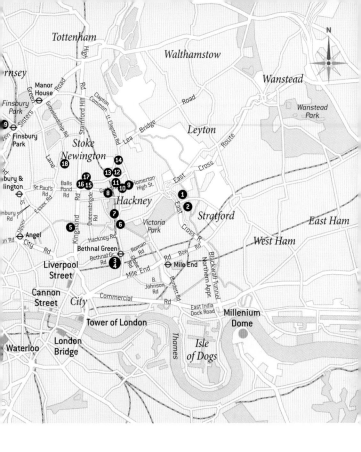

GROW, HACKNEY

De-sausaging the factory

98c Main Yard, Wallis Road, Hackney Wick, E9 5LN
020 8510 1757
grow-hackney.squarespace.com
hello@growhackney.co.uk
Wednesday and Thursday 12pm—12am, Friday and Saturday 12pm—2am,
Sunday 12pm—11pm
Rail/Tube station: Hackney Wick or Stratford

As we walk up the canal and through Hackney Wick, the streets are a maze of building sites and temporary boardwalks. Graffiti messages decorate the hoardings, telegraphing useful information, like

the fact that Nat not only suffers from a nasty trouser infection, but he also modifies his car for appearance not function. Either that or RICE is just something you eat, we can't quite decide. It feels a bit Wild East round here, but soon the hoardings will be torn down to reveal tightly fitted, expensive city flats that only allow those with dual incomes and a parental loan to get a foot on the London housing ladder.

And when that happens, Grow, Hackney will be under even more pressure to close down. It started off as an innocent, if slightly naive, way that a bunch of second-generation hippies could stay out of the rat race: by using their hands-on DIY skills to subdivide an old sausage factory into flats, studios and a music venue. It should have been easy: only basic planning permission and no neighbours to disturb – they could play their music as loud and late as they liked. But then the Olympics and the London Legacy developers moved in (aka The Man) and suddenly everything got horribly unhippyish. Legal and planning costs soared. The group had to sleep in the half-built warehouse over a freezing winter and work second jobs just to cover the lawyers' fees.

But they managed to finish it, albeit on the edge of a nervous breakdown. And in a brilliantly defiant way, they have created a laid-back bar and Berlin-style warehouse party venue. Enter through a small doorway at the bottom of an industrial cul-de-sac. Follow a pathway until you find yourself in a cavernous stage room with a bar at the side and a high skylight ceiling. Another doorway leads through a wide dark tunnel that doubles as a more secluded snug. Then up the steps, past a portacabin kitchen serving tasty grills, and you emerge onto a broad canal-side terrace which is a perfect hang-out on summer evenings.

Even outside, you get a great view of the bands below through the skylight windows. Sometimes they play on the water's edge.

Wednesday evenings are regular jazz sessions, and at weekends guest bands and DJs kick off the parties in the afternoon. By the time this book comes out it will be even more of an antithesis to the rapidly upscaling neighbourhood. But I, for one, hope they keep up the fight against The Man. Long live the hippies!

STOUR SPACE

Dust to dust

7 Roach Road, Tower Hamlets, E3 2PA
020 8985 7827
stourspace.co.uk
info@stourspace.co.uk
Monday–Wednesday 8am–5pm, Thursday and Friday 8am–late, Saturday and Sunday 9am–late
Rail/Tube station: Hackney Wick or Stratford
Buses: 276, 399, 488

It used to be really cheap to rent in Hackney Wick. Disused factories and warehouses, left over from the dyeing and printing industries, were not exactly habitable but they made perfect artists' studios. In the 1980s the area of Fish Island – so called because the streets bore the names of local fish: bream, dace and roach – began to swim with artists.

Soon they were found here in greater numbers than anywhere else in Europe. The once desolate post-industrial area began to thrive again. And then the 2012 Olympics came to London, together with the plan to regenerate East London. But instead of the regeneration continuing its organic process, it was rocket-fuelled by building incentives. Suddenly all the sites were bought up by developers, planning tightly packed

luxury flats with expensive rents. Thanks very much, artists, we don't need you any more. But some have resisted the developers' push. Stour Space, an artists' studio and gallery set up in 2009, is now surrounded by building sites.

You would only spot it if you were walking along the other side of the canal. Stour is Scots for "dust," and the idea is that the individual floating particles form a cloud – a collective who move together. They may be tiny, delicate but they are everywhere … The main area of the Stour Space warehouse is an open gallery space where you can see excellent exhibitions by local artists, often ranking in the top 5 of London shows.

On the first floor is a quiet room with huge windows, beautiful light and comfy battered armchairs – perfect for reading or writing. Downstairs, along the canal side, is a fantastic bohemian café, serving breakfasts, soups, sandwiches and cakes – all using local suppliers. You can sit inside by the window or, even better, outside on the wooden pontoon, watching canal boats drift by.

On a sunny morning, it is magical. And up in the rafters, supported by all this, are the artists' studios, with skylights, paint-splattered sinks and mezzanine walkways. Their affordable rents are subsidised by the profits from the café, yoga classes and event hire. So don't resist the delicious brunch, the cake or the homemade iced tea: your purchases are keeping the artistic community of Hackney Wick from biting the dust.

RENEGADE LONDON WINERY

London Sparkling

Arch 12, Gales Gardens, Bethnal Green, E2 0EJ
07502 991221
renegadelondonwine.com
warwick@renegadelondonwine.com
Wednesday–Friday 5pm–11pm, Saturday 2pm–11pm, Sunday 2pm–10.30pm
Tube/Rail station: Bethnal Green or Cambridge Heath

Down the back of the railway line at Bethnal Green tube station is a narrow alleyway rammed with second-hand furniture. Squeeze past

the wardrobes and bedside cabinets and you'll find some long benches which are not for sale, stretching across the front of two archways – an urban winery and a microbrewery – each fermenting drinks of very different character.

Renegade Winery was founded in 2016 by Warwick Smith, who wanted to escape the world of high finance and do something more creative. With a certain City-style swagger, he proceeded to hire an award-winning Kiwi wine technician, buy in top-quality grapes and use the latest technology to defy traditional terroir controls: mixing grapes from different countries, experimenting with yeast strains, ageing in not just oak but chestnut, cherry, even ex-bourbon barrels. The entire vinification process is done in this one archway. The walls are lined with stainless steel vats, rollers, wooden barrels and racks of stashed bottles, their labels designed by the winner of the annual artist competition. In the corner there's a huge pot-bellied *qvevri* – a ceramic Georgian vessel where whole bunches of grapes are fermenting on the stalk. Starting at £16 bottle/£6.50 a glass, the wines aren't so cheap – but come during happy hour or accompanied by a dog and you'll get a 15% discount. You can bring your own food along, so an evening doesn't have to be too pricey. If you get chatting to Warwick, he might challenge you to a bullish tasting game of "name that grape." Bacchus? Syrah? Pinot? Most distinctive is perhaps the Tempranillo, Grenache & Syrah mix in the Nat Fizz, an entirely natural sparkling rosé which ferments in the bottle.

NEARBY

Old Street Brewery

(4)

Arch 11, Gales Gardens, Bethnal Green, E2 0EJ
07491 990970
oldstreet.beer

A different fizz is brewing in the next archway down, at the Old Street Brewery tap room, where super-fresh ales are served directly from the tanks by the same guys who stir the beer pot: laid-back Arizonan Adam Green and Helsinki-born Andreas Wegelius. The misplaced name is because they started off in a kitchen by Old Street with a 20 litre all-grain brewing kit and a huge pile of books.

Their first commercial beer, sold the night Trump got elected, was called "Americas Finnished." Perhaps aided by the ominous election result, the beer went down so well they decided to take the plunge and open up their own microbrewery, still using the same original kit with a bit more steel welded on. It reminds me of the "Bia Hoi" fresh beer scene in Hanoi: lo-tech, low-falutin' and easy drinking. If you come by during the week you can see them brewing, and you're welcome to watch and learn, or help out. You'll soon work up a thirst.

THE KING'S HEAD

Taxidermorama

257 Kingsland Road, Hoxton, E2 8AS
020 7729 9419
thekingshead-london.com
emma@thekingshead-london.com
Tuesday 7pm—1am, Wednesday 7pm—3am, Thursday 7pm—4am, Friday and Saturday 7pm—5am
Membership required (see note below for special deal)
Overground station: Hoxton or Haggerston

As you walk up the Kingsland Road, you pass a pretty derelict-looking Irish pub, its shutters firmly down, paint peeling on the letters advertising "Pool, Darts and Setanta Sports." If that's what you're after, you're in the wrong place. Hidden behind this crumbling façade is a secret private members' club. But this is no Groucho or Blacks, it's more like walking into a still-life Serengeti.

Leaping over the top of the ground-floor bar is a huge ferocious liger – a cross between a lion and a tiger – frozen mid-pounce. The mounted heads of a rhino and a hippo peer out from the back wall. Climb the stairs – your hand brushing the vivid geometric print wall linen – and you will find more rooms, each more mind-blowing than the last. A polar bear rears up to his full height in the icy blue Regency drawing room.

A dining room is lined with 3,000 beautiful butterflies. A bathroom is fully occupied by four peacocks and a prowling tiger. Perched on the beams beneath the stairwell skylight is a static aviary filled with parrots, cockatoos and toucans. The last room at the top is perhaps the most extraordinary. A geometrically tiled bedroom strewn with wild cats – snow leopards, cheetahs, black panthers, lions and leopards. Snaking out of the ceiling are the huge neck and head of a giraffe – presumably the rest of her occupying the loft.

This spectacular safari was the vision of the owner, known to all as Rocky, who runs several bars around Shoreditch. He had amassed a huge collection of taxidermy – all antique and second hand – and wanted to showcase them somehow. But he couldn't just put them in a regular bar, there needed to be some way of protecting them. And given the high density of vegetarians in the Hoxton area, there would be many telling him to get stuffed. But a private members' club stops people just stumbling in, and also has the advantage of really late licensing hours. So Rocky set about converting the old pub, choosing the intensely decorative fabrics, furniture and tiles himself.

Though the list price might look a bit steep, you can get a special secret deal of £29 for annual membership if you tell them that you read about the wild cats in *Secret London: Unusual Bars & Restaurants* – the deal includes a pair of their delicious cocktails, so worth it even if you only go once. Dress flamboyantly and be ready for a wild night on the tiles.

THE LAST TUESDAY SOCIETY

A little louche

11 Mare Street, Hackney, E8 4RP
020 7998 3617
thelasttuesdaysociety.org
bookings@thelasttuesdaysociety.org
Tuesday 3pm–11pm, Wednesday–Saturday 12pm–11pm, Sunday 12pm –10.30pm
Events must be booked online
Tube/Rail station: Bethnal Green or Cambridge Heath

"Everything is improved by alcohol," declares Viktor Wynd, whose Museum of Curiosities, Fine Art & Natural History has been sponsored by Hendrick's Gin. And the entrance to his Hackney basement collection of the provocatively peculiar and titillatingly taboo is a place where one can procure just such improvements: a very fine cocktail bar named The Last Tuesday Society, run by New York/ London duo Allison Crawbuck and Rhys Everett.

Here, surrounded by unlikely skeletons and impossible animals, you can sip cocktails inspired by items in Wynd's collection: the "Jivaroan sour" is a version of the Pisco sour in honour of the Peruvian shrunken heads downstairs. "Happy and You Know It" is a delicious dark pink sour fizz named after a photograph of the London dandy Sebastian Horsley, whose scarlet sequinned suit is also on display. Or "Sex Instructions for Irish Farmers," a strong Irish twist on the Manhattan, in reference to a handy booklet to be found in another curious cabinet.

Or perhaps you would prefer to sample the powers of *la fée verte*? Absinthe is served in the traditional Belle Époque manner, with water dripped through a lump of sugar suspended over the glass on a perforated silver spoon – emulsifying the anise oils in the spirit, and turning it a milky green, the so called *louche* effect. You can develop a taste for it weeknights 6–7pm, during *l'heure verte*, a 19th-century precursor to the modern happy hour. Or you could attend the monthly "Absinthe drink and draw evening," where your subject might be wearing vintage lace and feathers or tied up Japanese *Shibari* style.

Feeling peckish? Share a platter of mixed insects – crunchy silkworms, queen ants, a cricket with a tiny mole's head and paws. An armour-tailed scorpion bursts unexpectedly in the mouth with a strong medicinal flavour, which thankfully turns out to be gin. To finish, you might enjoy a selection of chocolate anuses? The Society also throws food-tasting events such as the *Hallouminati* secret cheese evenings, and they were the proud hosts of the world's first sausage séance.

Or you can just grab a glass of vino and take a wander round the museum. It can only fit ten people at a time and is often booked up for events, so it's advisable to email or call ahead. Be prepared: you may require a stiff drink when you emerge.

MORTY & BOB'S

Room with a view

Second Floor, Netill House, 1–7 Westgate Street, London Fields, E8 3RL
020 3095 9420 (Buzz for entry)
www.mortyandbobs.com
hello@mortyandbobs.com
Monday–Friday 9am–5pm, Saturday and Sunday 10am–5pm
Tube station: London Fields
Bus: 55

We accidentally stumbled into a photo shoot while looking for this well-hidden staff canteen that morphs into a bar at weekends. Wedged between Broadway Market and Mare Street, Netil House is a drab 1960s' office block that was a community college, council offices and a squat before it became derelict for over a decade. The entrance to Morty & Bob's, via a grubby alleyway alongside a railway bridge, doesn't bode well either. But appearances can be deceptive.

Morty & Bob's is not your typical staff cafeteria, but the residents of Netil House are not your typical office workers. Pilates instructors, tattoo artists, illustrators and acrobats inhabit the studios leading off the green linoleum staircase, the last vestige of the building's institutional past. You can peek into the artists' studios during the day, or pretend you're one of

them in the second floor café. It's an unexpectedly huge space with scuffed concrete floors, a mash up of vintage furniture, and a wall of windows enjoying   fantastic views of the East London skyline. There's Canary Wharf to the left, the Gherkin and the Shard to your right. Sunsets from the terrace overlooking London Fields are spectacular. Trains chugging along the railway tracks at eye level give the scene a faintly futuristic edge.

There's a relaxed, improvised feel to everything from the sexy young staff to the simple, affordable food. Morty & Bob's started as a stall in next door's Netil market. They became famous for a very fine grilled cheese sandwich which is still on the menu, along with a weekly changing selection of organic, freshly prepared salads, sandwiches, soups and specials. On weekends they throw on a lively boozy brunch with a cocktail menu, top-notch egg dishes, and variations of their celebrated grilled cheese.

NEARBY
Wilton Way Café ⑧
63 Wilton Way, London Fields, E8 1BG
www.londonfieldsradio.com/café
London Fields Radio broadcasts live from a radio booth in the corner of this cute café, where all the furniture is fashioned from crates and corrugated iron.

I WILL KILL AGAIN

Split personality

Arch 216, 27a Ponsford Street, Hackney, E9 6JU
020 3774 0131
www.darkartscoffee.co.uk
info@darkartscoffee.co.uk
Friday–Sunday 10am–4.30pm
Overground/Rail station: Homerton or Hackney Central

Underneath the railway, half-way between Homerton and Hackney Central stations, down a "shitty lane" is an archway warehouse. On one side, bikers with long beards and tattoo sleeves roast and package coffee beans to thrash metal sounds and satanic exploitation movie posters. On the other side, young mums with babies on their knees are served flat whites, avocado stacks and vegan chocolate brownies by smiling baristas. Surely these are two different businesses forced to rent the same space? But then as you drain your cappuccino and see the words "I Will Kill Again" at the bottom, you realise this all part of one big happy scary family, kicked off by New Zealand couple Bradley Morrison and Talia Aitchison.

Brad and Talia met in a Brick Lane café where Brad was a barista and Talia his manager. Both had come to London by way of Melbourne and were inspired by the coffee scene there, which is even more intense than London's. Unimpressed by the blends served in Brick Lane, Brad challenged the owner that if he could improve on their beans, then they should switch suppliers. Being a motorbike enthusiast, Brad styled his new roasting biz around '70s motorbike culture, called it "Dark Arts Coffee", and gave the blends names like Lost Highway, Cult of Doom and Life After Death (decaf). Not only did they win the Brick Lane contract, they also developed a cult following with the heavy metal crowd. Then their friends kept dropping by and hanging out – it was obvious they should start a café. Talia is a vegan while Brad's a carnivore, and they always had problems finding somewhere they could both eat. So they decided to make really great veggie and vegan food, which can be augmented with dead things. "Not vegan?" asks one of their instaposts, "then drop some bacon and a fried egg on your quesadilla and stop ya whinging." Another explains they have options "for your vegan friend who insists on letting you know about every documentary on Netflix about meat production."

So under the same archway, and spilling onto tables outside, you'll find peace-loving animal rights hippies and road-killing petrolheads munching happily side by side. The wifi password is lordlucifer and the playlist alternates grunge and alt-country, metal and ambient as the staff from each side fight it out in the eternal battle between heaven and hell.

NEARBY

V Deli

Arch 215, Ponsfort Street, Hackney, E9 6JU
0208 127 1819
www.vdelicious.co.uk
In the archway next door, you'll find V Deli, where Kerry and her team make delicious vegan cupcakes, cookies and layer cakes that are dairy and egg-free.

BEHIND THIS WALL

Turning the tables

411 Mare Street, Hackney, E8 1HY
020 8985 3927
www.behindthiswall.com
alex@behindthiswall.com
Tuesday–Sunday 6pm–11 pm
Rail station: Hackney Central or Hackney Downs
Buses: 30, 38, 55, 48, 106, 236, 253, 276, D6, W15

"**B**ehind This Wall" was a piece of graffiti at Willesden Junction that Alex Harris passed every day on his way to his job teaching music technology. Then it was the name of a club night he ran. Then it was music pop-up events at which he became as good at mixing drinks as he was at spinning records. And now it's the name of his hidden basement bar, not really behind a wall, but down some inauspicious stairs on Hackney's recently widened Narrow Way. Once you finally find the right doorway, it's not the dark and dingy dive bar you might expect. Alex and his team built it themselves, turning the tables, chairs and bar out of pale plywood, which gives the room a light, minimalist Scandi feel. The DJ deck isn't in a corner behind a booth; the matching plywood plinth lowers down on ropes from the ceiling and hovers in the open space at just the right height. On it stand a single Technics turntable, a 1970s EAR preamp and a pair of glass valve amplifiers. Alex is an audio obsessive. The speakers were once owned by Martin Hannett, the brilliant but famously unstable Factory Records producer who found the distinctive sound for bands like Joy Division and the Happy Mondays. Serious record collectors come flying like bees to a honey-covered valve amp. They play an eclectic mix of jazz, soul, funk, hip-hop, house and maybe some techno. Surprisingly, you're allowed to ask them to turn it down if the music exceeds comfort levels – audiophiles have a tendency to suffer from hearing loss.

The cocktail ingredients are pretty niche too. They make their own syrups and juices, keeping everything as natural, fresh and low in sugar as possible. The drinks menu is seasonal – when I dropped by, it was spring and they had a seriously delicious homemade rhubarb and basil kombucha in the mix. The theory is that if you have fewer preservatives, colourings and sugar, then you'll get a more natural buzz and less of a hangover. Or you can hang the hangover altogether and go for their tasty temperance drinks. The best time to go is during happy hour from 6 to 8pm, when not only are there discounted drinks, but also oysters for £1 each. The best day to go is Sunday evening, when they hold their secret record launch parties. And perhaps the best house rule is that women should introduce themselves to men, not vice versa. Another table well turned.

PACIFIC SOCIAL CLUB

Whatever you fancy

8 Clarence Rd, Clapton, E5 8HB
07816 963127
www.pacificsocial.club
pacificsocialclub@gmail.com
Monday–Thursday 9am–4.30pm, Friday 9.30am–10.30pm, Saturday and
Sunday 9am–10.30pm (Drumsco pop up from 6pm Friday and Saturday)
Rail station: Hackney Central or Hackney Downs
Buses: 30, 38, 55, 48, 106, 236, 253, 276, D6, W15

Weekend nights are special at the Pacific Social Club. The café bar, hidden away on a residential street between Hackney and Clapton, is already pretty unique: matchboxes and record inner sleeves

line its walls; Japanese tin signage and Hawaiian Hula girls smile down at you. Weekdays the café has a laid-back, friendly bohemian feel, serving delicious toasties and brunchy sandwiches: the Venezuelan is a favourite, with morcilla, chorizo, black beans, avocado and cheese. There's a vegan version of the same thing – over half the menu is vegetarian or vegan. Laptops aren't allowed in the front room, so don't bury yourself in work. Look around, relax and chat. Or listen to whatever intriguing sounds are spinning on the turntables. See if you can figure out the musical genre. Was that '60s surfer Cumbia? And then maybe some Arabic gospel swing?

It is to sounds like these that on Fridays at 6pm, Drumsco ignite the griddle in the back room for their *okonomiyaki* pop up. Drumsco are Japanese drummers who also apply their creativity and precision to the kitchen. *Okonomiyaki,* meaning "whatever you fancy, grilled," are savoury pancakes which became popular in Japan when there was a rice shortage. There are two main styles, Osaka and Hiroshima. Here they cook the latter – a lighter, more layered version.

Handfuls of finely chopped cabbage, beansprouts and spring onions are coated in a thin flour batter and griddled until the surface is covered with crispy brown flecks. Then the toppings are piled on. We fancied all three varieties on offer: prawn, sweetcorn and crispy onion; pork, beansprout and shiso leaves; tomato, aubergine and parsnip. The pancakes arrive shimmering with flakes of pink bonito and sheath-cut spring onions, latticed with dark brown *okonomiyaki* sauce and creamy mayonnaise. My friend's teenage son perceptively describes them as a Japanese version of bubble and squeak – "but *loads* better".

We tuck into other yummy Drumsco hits. Crunchy spicy chicken *karaage*. Beautiful *inari* sushi: sweet beancurd pockets stuffed with rice, prawns, avocado and cucumber. Handmade pork *gyoza* fanned out on a crisp rice paper sheet – way more delicious and delicate than the standard noodle bar version. Then the evening's guest DJ arrives: Phil, the Man from Uranus, and the rest of the meal is taken up deciding if he's playing Martian pop psychedelia or electro cartoon dub …

NEARBY

Coffee Afrique

Pembury Centre, Atkins Square, 1 Dalston Lane, Hackney, E8 1FA
07984 526489
www.coffeeafrique.co.uk
On the ground floor of the Pembury Community centre, the lovely Simeera Hassan serves up fabulous spiced coffees and freshly made East African treats, along with inspiring workshops and wellness support.

MY NEIGHBOURS
THE DUMPLINGS

Hidden hanging garden

165 Lower Clapton Road, Hackney, E5 8EQ
020 3327 1556
myneighboursthedumplings.com
info@myneighboursthedumplings.com
Tuesday–Thursday 6pm–10.30pm, Friday 6pm–11pm, Saturday 5pm–11pm,
Sunday 5pm–9.30pm
Rail station: Clapton, Hackney Downs or Hackney Central

My Neighbours the Dumplings is a lovely fresh dim sum restaurant, run by young, hard-working couple Kris and Bec. As you might tell from the name, they're fans of Studio Ghibli animation. But they also wanted the restaurant, which started off as a pop-up, to have a neighbourhood feel. And it's worked: they're usually quite packed on a weekend evening, with the local Claptonites tucking into little baskets of handmade *sui mai* and *har gau*, or small plates of crispy lamb and coriander pot-stickers. To finish, there are less traditional chocolate dumplings: slim spring rolls filled with milk chocolate and served with a spoonful of salted caramel and a ball of stiff vanilla ice cream. The place is

busy, the kitchen is open and the music level is high.

But what many don't discover is the hidden hanging garden out the back. You have to go through Matilda's to get there – a basement sake bar named after their daughter, who was born one month after they opened (an accidental bit of timing, which they don't necessarily recommend). Behind the bar, premium craft sakes and oriental-influenced cocktails are on offer, accompanied by guest DJs or the occasional band. Kris used to play in a band called "One eskimo" so the couple have many musician friends. But keep going through the winding corridor and up the steps. And suddenly you emerge into another world. Diffuse light from the glass ceiling fills the room. Dark green plants line the rough red brick walls. Colourful glowing lanterns hang at different levels above long wooden bench tables. A huge monochrome print of the Panchen Lama by Tavares Strachen stares out from the back wall. High up, a toy train runs around a rooftop track. It's quite magical. The perfect place to sip one of the speciality teas, which arrive in glass pots with a little sand timer to ensure they're brewed just right.

When I looked around, it was just before opening time: the main table was being used by the chefs for a mass dumpling stuffing session. Kris was up in the main kitchen, prepping for service, and Bec, heavily pregnant with their second baby, was off to pick Matilda up from nursery. It feels like everyone is very hands on here. It may be a ten–fifteen minute walk from any of the area's overground train stations, but it's worth the trip …

LATTO'S PIZZA

Beside the curve

Dalston Eastern Curve Garden, 13 Dalston Lane, E8 3DF
dalstongarden.org
info@dalstongarden.org
Pizza oven operates summer weekends, May–September, approx. 2pm–9pm
Rail station: Dalston Kingsland or Dalston Junction

Dalston Eastern Curve Garden is a hidden green paradise behind a high wall, round the corner from the intense traffic stress of Dalston Junction. Step through the little doorway and emerge into a gladed silver birch wood, filled with flowers and wildlife, a pathway sweeping downwards and out of sight. The garden was established in 2010 on the curve of an old disused railway, creating a much-needed green community space in highly populated Hackney. The door is open 365 days of the year and welcomes all – you can bring your own food and sit at the picnic tables or on the sofas in the sheltered wooden pavilion area. In the winter there are blankets for you to wrap up warm and a little wood-fired stove in the greenhouse. But no need to pre-prepare: you can buy delicious seasonal home-cooked food and drinks from the café kiosk by the entrance, which is run as a social enterprise, so that the profits all go to the upkeep of the garden.

On weekdays you might notice a low yellow ochre igloo hiding in a back corner, walled off by a pile of logs, its front blackened by smoke. Come back on a summer weekend afternoon and you'll see it in action. This is the wood-fired pizza oven, which like much of the garden, was built in situ by local volunteers, including many from the local learning disabilities group. It is helmed by David Latto, who used to make sourdough pizzas in the ovens at the back of the nearby Palm2 hippy supermarket. Not only are the pizzas delicious, but you get to watch the whole mesmerising art of them being made up close. Stare into the furnace glow as the bread puffs, the cheese bubbles and the edges crisp before your pizza is swiftly fished out on a paddle and handed to you with freshly torn basil on top. There's not a huge list of toppings, just one or two options – maybe fresh mushroom, aubergine slices, or if you're lucky, artichoke hearts. The basic margarita only costs £6 and toppings a couple of quid more. Don't go expecting it all to run to set times – if it's a slow, overcast day they might not get the oven going until 3pm. But there are always people around to chat to and community events going on to distract you while you wait for some of the best pizzas in all London.

NEARBY

Dalston Roof Park (16)

18–22 Ashwin Street, E8 3DL
www.bootstrapcompany.co.uk/about-dalston-roof-park/

Climb the long stairs of the Bootstrap company's Print House – a task made easier by the hand-painted comic strip winding up the walls – and emerge onto an astro-turfed roof garden with great views, a barbecue shack at one end and a big club/dance bar at the other, with a retractable roof if the sun don't shine. Thursdays to Sundays they have ticketed events in the evenings with big name DJs, but Wednesdays are free community events like film screenings and fundraisers.

DUSTY KNUCKLE

Bread winner

Bootyard, Abbot Street Car Park, Dalston, E8 3DP
020 3903 7598
www.thedustyknuckle.com
enquiries@thedustyknuckle.com
Tuesday–Friday 8.30am–3.30pm, Saturday and Sunday 9am–3.30pm
Rail station: Dalston Junction or Dalston Kingsland

The Dusty Knuckle Bakery is down the end of a very unpromising-looking alleyway at the back of the Arcola Theatre. As you enter the Bootyard, you'll see a blue shipping container ahead with the words "Dusty Knuckle" printed on the side. You may be relieved to know that this isn't it. It is where they started though, answering a Bootstrap competition for local startups. Max Tobias and Becca Oliver only found out about it the day before the deadline. But their entry for a high-end bakery that would train and employ troubled young people was a proper bread winner.

Max became a bread head when at the age of 13 he made his first loaf for his granddad's funeral. It was, by his own admission, a bit crummy – but the feeling of accomplishment and the praise he received got him hooked. Later, working in conflict mediation with kids with severe emotional and behavioural difficulties, he was frustrated by the limitations of the charity sector. A bakery could offer proper employment in a respectable working environment. The hours are early, the work is physical, but the routine – day 1 mix, day 2 bake – creates structure and self-respect. And you get to see your cooperation and hard graft immediately rewarded by something tangible and a little bit magical: flour and water turned into delicious crusty sourdough loaves.

Soon the business was outgrowing the shipping container – which had the added ingredient of sub-zero winters and 40-degree summers (not good for a craft which relies on the delicate process of natural fermentation). So they de-tinned into the space opposite: a proper building with solid brick walls, even temperatures and room enough not just to bake and dispatch, but also to run a café.

So before you hit the blue shipping container, turn right and you'll find a spacious open café/bakery. If you appear before 9am, the entire floor is dedicated to packing and loading up vans for the wholesale business. But after that you can get fantastic breakfasts and pastries (their sticky buns are the bee's knees) and at lunchtime, there are delicious salads, soups and sandwiches. And of course amazing bread. Plain or seeded sourdough, tangy rye, chewy potato, sweet raisin and walnut, rich focaccia. Well worth spending your dough on.

NEARBY
Luminary Bakery

71–73 Allen Road, Stoke Newington, Hackney, N16 8RY
www.luminarybakery.com
The Luminary Bakery is a sort of soul sister to the Dusty Knuckle, training women from troubled backgrounds to make amazing cakes and pastries in their deli/café hidden in a back street halfway between Dalston and Stoke Newington (and they also sell Dusty Knuckle bread).

OAK N4

Top shelf

5–7 Wells Terrace, Finsbury Park, N4 3JU
020 7684 1294
www.oakn4.co.uk
wines@oakn4.co.uk
Sunday–Monday 12pm–10pm, Tuesday–Thursday 12pm–11pm, Friday and
Saturday 12pm–12am
Tube station: Finsbury Park

The back of Finsbury Park station isn't the most obvious place to open a wine bar and shop. Everyone is in a rush to get out of there. The streets around are mainly wholesale fashion trade and many of the locals are teetotal on religious grounds. Or because they're toddlers (there's a crèche next door). Though in fact, unusually for a wine bar, OAKN4 is pretty-child friendly – Helena and Cameron, who set it up, have young children themselves so they understand the pressures.

The actress friend who joins me also has two young children – but has cunningly managed to ditch them with a neighbour, so is in celebration mode at the prospect of an uninterrupted adult sentence. We sit and catch up at the huge long copper-topped bar and taste some

really interesting wines from the seasonally changing range they serve by the glass. My friend is very excited to find Grüner Veltliner whites and I am enchanted by a Georgian orange. And as somebody in whom sulphites induce a not-so-glamorous sneezing fit, I also love that they stock so many natural wines. The actress and I have only just got into the proper adult chat when she realises her babysitting time is up. She seriously considers using her professional skills to invent a dramatic excuse – but guilt gets the better of her and suddenly she's off, stopping only to buy a bottle to go (and I don't think it's for the neighbour).

I am left in the capable hands of Sicilian wine expert Pino to experience the "wine flight tastings" they organise, starting at £15 a head. He's very friendly and low key, giving me an excellent education in how to select the kinds of wine I like. Such as the simple fact that the shape of the bottle is an indication of the character of the wine within. A straighter silhouette preserves the freshness of young wines, while wider, squarer shoulders are designed to trap sediment left in higher tannin, fuller bodied wines.

This is all part of OAKN4's mission to demystify wine. To that end, the shelves are laid out not by country but by character. As you move along them from left to right. the wines get fuller in body, more complex in flavour. And the higher up you go, the pricier – toddler-level bottles kick off at £11 while the on tip-toes stuff starts at £40 and goes well over £100. Maybe one day I'll be grown up enough to reach it.

SHAYONA

Palate cleanser

54—62 Meadow Garth, Neasden, NW10 8HD
020 8965 3365
www.shayonarestaurants.com
info@shayonarestaurants.com
Monday—Friday 12pm—10pm, Saturday—Sunday 11am—10pm
Tube station: Stonebridge Park, Neasden or Harlesden then 10-15 minute-walk
Bus: 224

There's one very good reason to make a pilgrimage to Neasden, surely one of London's dreariest suburbs. Shri Swaminarayan Mandir, the largest Hindu temple outside India, is as much a tribute to Indian stonemasonry as to its spiritual guru, Bhagwan Swaminarayan. No metal was used in the temple's construction, only marble, limestone and wood. For two years, over 1,500 Indian craftsmen worked night and day to sculpt the seven pinnacles, six domes, and 26,300 pieces of intricately carved stone. Every piece was numbered and shipped in 160 containers to London, where the temple was assembled like a giant jigsaw puzzle.

A spry 98-year-old volunteer was on cloakroom duty when I visited. He was the perfect poster-boy for following a *sattvic* diet, which eschews spicy, salty and pungent foods such as onions and garlic, on the grounds that they agitate the mind, causing lust and cravings for material possessions. Easy to digest, *sattvic* foods are said to purify the mind and body, bringing a sense of clarity, compassion and contentment (Paul

McCartney ordered *sattvic* snacks for his wedding to Heather Mills, but judging by their acrimonious divorce this didn't have the desired effect).

Shayona, a charitable restaurant that raises funds for the temple and Hindu community, is the only pure *sattvic* restaurant in London. Across the road and through the temple car park, the entrance is via an Indian food store, with a mind-boggling array of (suspiciously spicy) Bombay mix and frozen pakoras. Beyond the day-glo sweet counter is a large dining room with an all-you-can-eat buffet. The back room is more formal, with wood-panelled walls, fake flowers, and a menu that covers the sub-continent.

Well-fed Indian families were tucking into Gujurati *thalis* and Keralan *dosas* on a midweek afternoon (weekends are busiest, both in the restaurant and temple). There's no alcohol, only fresh juices or delicious mango lassi. Starters of samosas, bhajias and bel puris tend towards the deep-fried. A selection of dishes from Northern India was equally rich: Shayona Shahi Paneer (cheese in creamy saffron sauce), Dal Makhani (a beautifully buttery blend of mixed pulses), and Shayona Jeera (cumin rice), all scooped up with ghee-soaked nan bread.

According to *sattvic* principles, meals should be eaten between sunrise and sunset and you should only fill three-quarters of your stomach, leaving space for water and air. I certainly hadn't left any room for sweet *gulabjambus* and *rassomalais*, drenched in syrup and condensed milk.

Time your visit to coincide with evening prayers in the mandir, when monks chant mesmerising mantras before their idols, whose elaborate outfits are changed several times a day.

ACE CAFE LONDON

Better than Little Chef

Ace Corner, North Circular Road, Stonebridge, NW10 7UD
020 8961 1000
www.london.acecafe.com
Monday–Saturday 7am–11pm (7am–2am when operating as a nightclub),
Sunday and public holidays 7am–10.30pm
Tube station: Stonebridge Park

"Mostly we host petrol," says Mark Wilsmore. "On a warm night, there might be 5,000 bikes parked outside."

For a man whose twin obsessions are motorbikes and rock and roll, Wilsmore has a dream job. He runs the Ace Café, a classic pit stop built in 1938 to cater for drivers using the new North Circular Road. A glamorous precursor of the motorway service station, there were petrol pumps, a "washmobile" that cost a whopping five shillings, car showrooms, and a restaurant, where football teams who played at Wembley ate after a match. Greasy truck drivers would refuel at the cafe next door.

Bombed during the war, the Ace Cafe was rebuilt in 1949. Open 24 hours, it soon became a magnet for teenage motorcyclists who raced up and down the motorway. There was no speed limit in those days; daredevils would drop a coin into the jukebox and race to a given point before the

song ended. Rock and roll was banned from radios in the 1950s, so the Ace's jukebox was an attraction in its own right (the juke box still plays some classic '50s tracks in amongst the hard rock and heavy metal). "It was the birth of youth culture," says Wilsmore. "But they didn't serve booze back then, only mugs of strong tea and doorstop sandwiches."

The Ace Cafe closed in 1969. Subsequently used as a filling station, bookmaker, and tyre depot, the building remained pretty much intact. When Wilsmore organised a reunion in 1994 over 12,000 people turned up. He set up a burger shack on site, eventually bought the freehold and reopened the café in 2001.

Today, the setting – on a motorway service road opposite an industrial estate – doesn't exactly ooze glamour. Back then, the whole area would have reeked of vinegar from the Heinz factory nearby. Now, it smells of biscuits baking at the McVitie's factory. Yet nostalgic rockers, bikers, mods and Teddy boys continue to flock to this vintage-themed greasy spoon and "one-stop rockers' shop." Ageing rockabillies in leather jackets and greying quiffs come for the Gene Vincent and Eddie Cochran tribute bands. One day, the forecourt will be inundated with bearded beefcakes on Harleys, the next with sharply dressed mods and vintage Minis.

"The Ace has an almost religious significance for many people from all different demographics," says Wilsmore. "The bikes and the music may have changed, but the spirit remains the same."

BASRAH LOUNGE

Hooked on hookahs

165 Dukes Road, Park Royal, W3 0SL
020 8752 1341
basrahlounge.co.uk
info@basrahlounge.co.uk
Sunday—Thursday 2pm—12.45am, Friday and Saturday 2pm—1.45am
Tube station: Park Royal

I am not an aficionado of shisha lounges – I don't even smoke – but my friend Ahmed does and he loves this place. Getting there is a bit of an adventure. Driving in the dark of night, you take a slightly nerve-wracking double slip road off the A40 behind the Park Royal Vue cinema, and turn down a crumbling road into the industrial shadows. There are a few lorries parked alongside the spiked railings, but as you get closer, more and more flashy four-by-fours, with a smattering of personalised number plates. At the end a doorman guards the entrance to a black shuttered warehouse. Ahmed tells me the password is "We are your friends and we have no knives," but thankfully I work out that he's joking and just smile politely.

The doorman lifts the red rope and suddenly we're in a *Blade Runner* set. Turquoise neon lights stripe the ceiling and recede into the distance, their lines only interrupted by giant screen TVs currently showing the same duplicated talking head. The white marble floor reflects the effect, and mirror-tiled pillars break it into thousands of tiny squares. Rows and rows of black leather VIP seats are stationed around low tables. The place is vast.

Our seats are below huge vertical LED chandeliers, bathing us in slowly changing electric colours. The Arabic pop music is quite loud but seems to float above us, so we can still chat to each other. Everywhere are groups of young men and women of all ethnicities – relaxing, playing games, sharing food and shisha pipes. It must be well air-conditioned as there's no low fug and no smell of smoke. Ahmed tells me the shisha here is good quality – smooth and non-chemical. But it's still like smoking 40 fags, so I'm only watching as one of the waiters ladles hot charcoals from a copper pan onto the silver hookah pipe.

People around us are eating a mix of traditional Arabic mezze and Americana fast foods, though the menu is very international and has lots of great non-alcoholic drinks and sumptuous sweet pastries. At one point the music turns to infectious Egyptian pop and a sparkling birthday cake is accompanied by a group of handsome clapping waiters. A major improvement on dreary renditions of "Happy Birthday." I think I prefer this to the pub culture I grew up with – more relaxed, less drunken and less Scotch eggs. Just be careful you don't develop a shisha and sugar habit instead.

THE WALPOLE

Southern Ealing comfort

35 St Mary's Road, Ealing, W5 5RG
020 8567 7918
walpole-ealing.co.uk
Messaging via facebook.com/TheWalpoleEaling
Friday and Saturday 7pm–10.30pm
Tube station: South Ealing or Ealing Broadway
Bus: 65

As you walk down from the high street chains of Ealing Broadway, the busy urban centre seems to drift back in time to the old English village it once was. And there on the left is what looks like a little old English café, with red gingham curtains and the name of Britain's first prime minister, Walpole, in white capitals on pillar-box red paint.

But the little swing sign in the door tells you it's closed. If you pass by during the week, you might be forgiven for thinking the owners were away on perpetual holiday – but what you need to do is book in on a Friday or Saturday night. Because that's when husband and wife team Wendy and Louis open their doors for the slap-up suppers they've been prepping all week.

The couple live above the restaurant, source all their ingredients from the London markets, and make everything on their short set menu from scratch: the bread, the 12-hour slow-cooked meats, the ice creams, the shortbreads, the pear marmalade. The only things they don't make are the condiments, because they reckon you can't beat Coleman's for mustard or mint sauce.

And they're not stingy. Our starters include a deep tureen of delicious crab bisque topped with a small mountain of Parmesan, and a log pile of colossal green asparagus with a gravy boat full of stiff hollandaise. The main courses come with a warning from Wendy that they do doggy bags because her husband is Greek Cypriot and so has a slight problem with portion control. My huge hunk of slow roast Romney Marsh lamb leaves almost no room on the plate for the piles of creamy mash and sugar-glazed carrots. My friends' dishes are laden with so much pappardelle that they are defeated less than half-way through. We don't have room for dessert or any more wine, but our hosts insist on topping up our glasses and treating us with some golf-ball-sized homemade truffles.

It really feels like you're a guest in their home. The back corridor is lined with crayon drawings that children (and some adults) have made on the brown paper tablecloths as they while away their happy time. We arrived at 7pm but at 10pm we're still sitting chatting merrily, and realise that the reason it's so relaxed is because there's only one sitting. "You can stay as long as you like," says Wendy, who has been known to come down in her pyjamas to lock up. Just as well – after all that comfort food, we may need to stay the night.

ACKNOWLEDGEMENTS

Gill Roth & Andrew Clarke, Jeremy & Hilary Redhouse, Jan Pearson, Susan Husband,
Marion Vivien, Sheryn Omeri, Jeremy Vincent & Helen Woodward, Indra Khanna,
Jez Benstock, Lila & Eli Rawlings, Dimitar Christoff, Peter McQuillan & Lucinda Thomson,
Giselle Whiteaker, Beth McHattie, Andry Anastasis-McFarlane, Catriona Pollock, Bruce Marcus,
Cassie Delaney-Brown & Anne-Marie McGrath, Teresa Whitter, Yasser Benj, Jess Boyde, Gaby Agis,
Bill Nash, Angelos Talentzakis ...
Thank you for sharing all your secrets and appetites!

PHOTOGRAPHY CREDITS

Photographs graciously provided by the locations themselves and by the following photographers:
Joakim Blockstrom, Addie Chinn, Peter Dazely, Hanson Leatherby, Rachel Megawhat, Jorge
Monedero, Jan Pearson, Yogesh Ram, Hannah Robinson, Carla Romero, Mona Sosa, Steve Ullathorne

Maps: Cyrille Suss - **Layout design:** Coralie Cintrat - **Layout:** Alessio Melandri and Emmanuelle
Willard Toulemonde - **Copy-Editing:** Jana Gough - **Proofreading:** Caroline Lawrence, Kimberly
Bess and Eleni Salemi - **Publishing:** Clémence Mathé